REAL

THE POWER OF AUTHENTIC CONNECTION

CATHERINE O'KANE, MA, RCC, RCS
DUANE O'KANE, RCC, RCS

Book Cover Design: Marla Thompson, Duane O'Kane
Book Cover Photo: Duane O'Kane
Typeset: Greg Salisbury
Portrait Photographer: Duane O'Kane

Dedication

To Erin, our greatest teacher, experimental subject, and daughter. Thank you for being the biggest part of this story (since 1994), both in terms of living it and helping us write it.

"*Real* isn't how you are made," said the Skin Horse. "It's a thing that happens to you. When a child loves you for a long, long time, not just to play with, but REALLY loves you, then you become Real."

"Does it hurt?" asked the Rabbit.

"Sometimes," said the Skin Horse, for he was always truthful. "When you are Real you don't mind being hurt."

"Does it happen all at once, like being wound up," he asked, "or bit by bit?"

"It doesn't happen all at once," said the Skin Horse. "You become. It takes a long time. That's why it doesn't happen often to people who break easily, or have sharp edges, or who have to be carefully kept. Generally, by the time you are Real, most of your hair has been loved off, and your eyes drop out and you get loose in the joints and very shabby. But these things don't matter at all, because once you are Real you can't be ugly, except to people who don't understand."

—**Margery Williams**, *The Velveteen Rabbit*

Today you are you! That is truer than true! There is no one alive who is you-er than you!

—**Dr. Seuss**

In practical and sensible detail this compact volume reveals the three basic principles of human health and happiness: connection, vulnerability and self-responsibility. Real is a helpful primer for all those on the healing path, and for those who seek to guide others towards wholeness.

Gabor Maté, MD, Author of *In the Realm of Hungry Ghosts: Close Encounters with Addiction*

Anyone considering therapy or ... anyone who is offering it will treasure this book—so comprehensive, relevant, quotable, practical, doable and inspirational.

Joanie Tara, President of the Association of Cooperative Counselling Therapists of Canada

I've known Catherine for many years and Duane for many decades. Together they are an incredible pair of "angels." They have the experience, wisdom and method to help each individual with our life problems, and in doing that, we all can help ourselves and friends and families around us. Their book, Real, is a must for everyone of all ages to read and keep on the shelf as an instruction manual. We can create our own universe around us and have the ability to control our destiny. What's the silver bullet? The magic pill? It's inside each of us, and Duane and Catherine are exceptionally great at helping each of us find ourselves, our path, and teach[ing] us how to follow it. It's not easy, it's not light... It's heavy stuff but it works. It's REAL.

Randy Bachman, Host of CBC Radio's Vinyl Tap and Canadian musician best known as lead guitarist, songwriter, and founding member of the 1960s and 70s rock bands The Guess Who and Bachman-Turner Overdrive.

In this book, Duane and Catherine identify a primary need of all human beings—connection. They provide a model of awareness and communication that transforms conflict and separation into shared understanding and connection. Personal real-life examples illustrate the effectiveness of this way of being.
Mahmud Nestman, Counsellor and Director of the Cura Institute for Integrated Learning

Having run an A Course in Miracles–based organization and magazine for 22 years, I can highly recommend Duane and Catherine's work. It is deeply inspired by the Course and brings those principles to life in a dynamic, immediate and life-changing way.
Ian Patrick, Editor of *Miracle Worker* magazine

ACKNOWLEDGEMENTS

We have a tremendous amount of gratitude for many people who have contributed to our work and this book. Thank you to our families, particularly our parents, Bob, Audrey, and Lorraine, for your love and support and for understanding that your story is part of our story.

We have the best staff in the world! Thank you to our teaching and facilitating team for your love and creative input into our work. Thank you to our administration team for your unwavering support and patience when it takes days or weeks to get a response from us. Thank you to our marketing and promotions team for your absolute faith in what we do. Most of all, thank you, everyone, for your friendship.

To all our clients, both individual and the many who attend our group workshops, your courageous vulnerability is inspiring! Thank you for continuing to ask for this book: your persistence finally paid off. Hopefully it has lived up to your expectations. To Julie Salisbury and the Influence Publishing team, we appreciate your skill and support as we navigate through this new literary territory.

We are grateful for the many personal and professional mentors who have impacted us, particularly Mahmud Nestman and Dale Trimble. Duane would also like to acknowledge Philip Mistleberger and Sandy Levey for their partnership and support in the early 1990s, as well as Robert Perry and Allen Watson for their mindful influence.

Contents

Introduction

Catherine, every time you ask me if I know what time I am going to be home, I have to visit the home I came from first. When you seem unhappy I feel like a failure, just like my dad. That is where my upset really is. I didn't know that. I have been punishing you now for what happened to me back then. That isn't fair. I have no right to do that. You had nothing to do with it. I am sorry.

All you want to do is create a home for us. I am so scared of what you will find in me, that I am a failure, like my dad... defective. I run, hide, and blame you for any of the problems, including accusing you of being needy. That is wrong and irresponsible. I have a problem. This is my problem. I am finally taking responsibility for what is my pain. I love you. You will never hear me suggest to you ever again that you are the explanation for my pain.

This is a book about connection. There is now an abundance of well-constructed long-term research that shows unequivocally that human beings are happier, healthier, and live longer when we have strong relationships. We are at our best when we are living a connected life, surrounded by people we love and care about. Unfortunately, these studies often conclude with some very light suggestions on how to build a strong relationship network. The solution to the problem of disconnection is more complex than bringing flowers home for your partner, or picking up the phone to connect with a relative you haven't spoken to in a while.

Despite the fact that technology apparently has us more connected than in any other time in history, we are suffering in isolation. We don't know how to connect, and the ways we go about attempting to do so more often contribute to the problem. The lack of authentic connection permeates the very fabric of how we organize ourselves in the modern world. It explains and contributes more to our personal malaise, work issues, high divorce rates, mental illness, and physical sickness than any other factor. The violence, terrorism, and militant religious wars that erupt in our cities and world on a daily basis are more a result of a polarized and separated population than what is cited as the cause in the war rooms.

> We aren't avoiding each other because of the problems. We have problems because we are avoiding each other. We aren't separate because of the wars. We have wars because we are separate.

When we feel disconnected, anything goes and usually does. We don't care about the impact on another because we do not know who the other is. We aren't avoiding each other because of the problems. We have problems because we are avoiding each other. We aren't separate because of the wars. We have wars because we are separate. The price we will continue to pay both personally and globally in our separate state is staggering and predictable. It is time we learned to care again.

This is a challenging task for the human psyche now that we have moved beyond our "villages" into the global arena. But how we play our "villages," our own immediate web of connections, will inform how we connect in the global arena. The rewards for becoming a connected and emotionally responsible human being living in an emotionally responsible world cannot be measured. Connection is how we return to our most natural and magnificent loving state.

HAPPINESS IS A BYPRODUCT, NOT A GOAL

What do you really want in your life? People will respond to this question in many different ways, but the most common answer is "I want to be happy." The underlying premise that "happiness" is a worthy goal in life creates all kinds of psychological suffering. Do you actually know anyone who you would say is happy all the time, or even most of the time? Happiness is a transient emotion, one that is humanly unsustainable.

The premise that individual happiness is the ultimate goal of living gets us into all kinds of trouble, because it leads to an endless cycle of pursuit and disappointment. It starts in a moment of unhappiness. We ruminate about what it is going to take to fix this terrible feeling, and we identify some *thing* outside of self to pursue, in the misguided belief that if we get that thing we will be happy. A better job/body/outfit/car/house/life/partner. You just have to flip through a magazine at the checkout stand to be tempted by the promise that external things will bring happiness.

And yet, the promise never delivers. We might get the thing we think we need but end up disillusioned because it doesn't bring happiness. At most, things provide a moment of pleasure, which is nice, but when the pleasure fades, we decide we didn't pick the right thing and embark on a new pursuit. Equally, we might suffer because we don't get the thing we think we need.

We might be a little more enlightened about what we believe will bring us happiness and embark on a path of "self-improvement." Now, there is nothing wrong with seeking to be a better person; that, to some degree, is what this book is all about. Self-improvement aiming towards "happiness," however, can easily become destructive perfection-seeking. When the immediate high attached to personal development fades, we decide that our "improvement" didn't work, and we escalate our efforts. We embark on another cycle of pursuit and disappointment. The promise never delivers.

Self-improvement also has as its premise that satisfaction in life comes from actualizing our individual potential. Western culture in particular has been aggressively selling this for well over half a century now. The "American dream" is but one variation of the promise that happiness comes from pursuing and satisfying our individual ambitions in life. Ironically, as an adult population we are more depressed, overweight, addicted, medicated, and in debt than at any other time in history.

There is a bigger, more worthy goal for us to aspire to as human beings, an experience that we all long for, and that is connection. There have literally been thousands of Attachment Theory–based books written about the human need for connection. Connection gives meaning and purpose to our lives. We all want to belong, to love and be loved. It is time to let go of our individualistic frame of reference and realize that the experience we long for is a collective one.

Those on their deathbeds consistently report regretting the time they spent in pursuit of money or things. What is of most concern to them is love given and love received. Most evaluate their lives from the perspective of love, asking themselves, "Have I loved well? Do the people I love know that I love them? Have I had a positive impact? Will I be remembered well?" When all the layers are peeled away, this is the desire we are left with at the core.

Just as fitness is a byproduct of exercise, happiness is a by-product of loving, relational action.

Just as fitness is a byproduct of exercise, happiness is a byproduct of loving, relational action. If we aim for connection as our goal, loving action is the way to get there. If we learn how to legitimately connect, we will find ourselves having many moments of happiness as a byproduct. The experience of connection transcends happiness, encompassing the whole spectrum of human experience. In connection we might feel pain, because pain is inevitable in our life experience, but pain felt when held, metaphorically or literally, in loving arms can be quite beautiful. We suffer in solitude, in the state of disconnection or isolation. Suffering, as Haruki Murakami said, is optional.

The quality of our life experience shifts dramatically when we make connection our goal, on a psychological, emotional, and spiritual level. We move from pursuing the narrow feeling of "happiness" on the emotional spectrum to experiencing what it means to be fully alive and fully human. We may not be happy all the time, but life has a strong pulse and is rich. Within the context of connection, we discover that we can be who we are, flaws and all. Our ability to meet, accept, and embrace our flaws is what will save our relationships, as opposed to ruin them. We experience the rainbow of human emotion, rather than just pursuing a narrow sliver of it. There is nothing to fear, because we belong and are good enough as we are.

This book is about you and for you. It all starts with you. You are here to be yourself, to be authentic, loving, vulnerable, brave, and honest. You can do no more in this life, and hopefully by the time you complete this book, you will do no less. If we can help you learn to reflect rather than reload, and to truly show up in all your relationships, then there will be one more real person helping the world to do the same.

We are both Registered Clinical Counsellors who have

been in the helping profession for over 60 years collectively. The wisdom we offer here comes first and foremost from our personal experience. You will get to know us through these pages, as even in the writing we are attempting to demonstrate what we teach. What we offer also comes from the relationships we have established all over the world with clients and workshop participants who, through their courageous transparency, have helped us hone our approach to a science. Their stories appear in these pages as well, and we hope and trust that you will see yourself mirrored here and be shown the way through your own struggle. We all deserve to live in connection.

PART ONE: UNREAL

The most important kind of freedom is to be what you really are. You trade in your reality for a role. You trade in your sense for an act. You give up your ability to feel, and in exchange, put on a mask. There can't be any large scale revolution until there's a personal revolution, on an individual level. It's got to happen inside first.
—Jim Morrison

There's no reality except the one contained within us. That's why so many people live an unreal life. They take images outside them for reality and never allow the world within them to assert itself.
—Herman Hesse

1 Problems Start in Relationships (The Past)

Reporter, to Einstein: What is the most important question facing humanity today?
Einstein: Is the universe a friendly place, or not?

If you think about it, how you answer this question for yourself will determine how you walk through your life. Do you see your life as an exciting adventure? Can't wait to get out of bed in the morning, to greet the endless, open possibility of the day ahead of you, like a two-year-old? Or are you governed by caution and fear, concerned about protecting yourself and anxious about what lies ahead? We are all set up to operate at some level from fear, and what we extend into our relationships then plays out in predictable ways, as we shall see.

The suffering we experience in life has more to do with our inability to authentically connect than anything else, but we do not explain it to ourselves that way. We prefer to explain our pain with "him or her or this or that": we prefer to keep the explanation outside ourselves. If only my partner talked to me more/had more sex with me/gave me space... If only my boss appreciated me/gave me a raise/promoted me... If only my family wasn't so dysfunctional/lived closer to me/lived in another country... If only him or her or this or that was different, then I would be fine.

We prefer to see the problem as something outside ourselves, but therefore the solution must be outside ourselves as well. Therein lies the dilemma. If the problem and the solution are outside of self, then we are doomed to be victims of the effects of external causes ultimately beyond our control. If the problem and the solution are within, then we can change.

The real problem is what we are holding at an emotional level, in what we refer to as the "basement" of our psyches, and because of that, how we position ourselves in relationship to others. The solution is to address both what we believe and how we extend those beliefs to the world around us. Both are necessary: the what (in the basement) and the how (in connection).

YOU ARE CONNECTED ALL THE TIME: THERE IS NO CHOICE

The first thing we need to understand around the problem of connection is that we are already connected. Despite our culture glorifying individuality, we define and experience self through relationships with others. No matter how we position ourselves in relationships, whether we are distant, cut off, intimate, reactive, or fused, it doesn't matter. We have a choice about how we connect, but we do not have a choice about whether we connect.

From birth we are connected through active emotional channels with everyone whom we have had contact with, particularly of any significant nature. We are not individuals, not in the sense of being truly separate: we are individuals who live in the context of an active, living web of influence through relationships. We cannot be understood in isolation from one another, because we define ourselves and shape our identities in relationship to others. The influence others (and we) exert is constant. Picture yourself in the centre with lines or channels connecting you to everyone, past and present, in your life. These channels are active all the time.

It may at first be hard to grasp the concept that we have an active, present emotional connection with everyone we have been in any kind of significant contact with, regardless of whether they are currently part of our lives. Take a moment, for example, to think of your first love, or your best friend from high school. What happens? Whatever the nature of your emotional response, that feeling influences you, and wherever in the world that person is now, they are also influenced by you.

Social media in particular allows us the illusion that we actually can cut and run. Deleting someone we know from Facebook or our contacts makes us believe that we can actually delete a relationship. Can we just unplug someone? No. Even with the action of deleting someone, we are injecting that message into the line or channel between us: "I am deleting you."

If you don't have a choice whether or not you are in relationship, then what choices remain? Your choice is about how you connect. How you connect is the strongest determinant of how you feel, and how you connect exerts a powerful influence on all those around you.

Content and relationship messages

We cannot *not* communicate. Connection is active all the time, with every thought, every word, every action. Not communicating is communicating. We are communicating all the time and are connected all the time. There are no neutral moments or situations.

Every time we actively communicate, there are two levels to that communication: there is the content or literal message, but underlying that is a relationship message that is conveyed mostly non-verbally, through body language, facial expression, and tone of voice. In terms of the impact of a communication on the receiver, the content of the message is worth about 20% of the communication, while the relationship level is responsible for 80%. The relationship message always overrides the content: you cannot lie at a relationship level! What you are really feeling always comes through, and when what you say with your words doesn't match the relationship message, people will respond to the relationship message.

This is why commercials for prescription drugs actually work. Despite the majority of the spoken content of such commercials firing dire warnings about the side effects of the medication, including death, all is said in a pleasant tone of voice while we watch pictures of smiling, happy faces. The relationship message overrides the content.

We are impacting others all the time with what we believe about self, other, and the world through our relationship web. How could we not? We do this by the manner we sit, talk, don't talk, walk, and behave. We are always conveying a message about the relationship we are in or avoiding. These messages are active and always. They do not sleep.

I could be chatting to you for a brief instant in a coffee bar in line waiting to order my latte. We could have an apparently innocuous chat about the rain that we both just walked out of. On a content level (20%), we have exchanged information about the weather. But the instant contact is made, I also fill this newly formed connective channel with my beliefs about self, other, and the world. If I believe that I do not matter and am of no interest to anyone, that people are insensitive and are only concerned with what they can get from me, and that the world at large is a dog-eat-dog place, this will be communicated on a relationship level. Thoughts and beliefs such as these are not neutral, dormant, sitting by themselves on an island inside my head. They are active as hell—or heaven. These are the thoughts and beliefs that I brought into the café before I met you. They are eager to prove themselves.

I might transmit this by avoiding eye contact or making the conversation as short as possible, thus conveying the message that I do not trust you. I might broadcast my lack of trust through my dispassionate tone of voice, my darting eyes, looking at my watch, or worse agitation. I will present this by disqualifying, disagreeing, or dismissing your assessment of the weather in some way. As much as we have no choice whether we are communicating or not, the person on the other end also has no choice whether they are a receiver. That person will walk away feeling a little anxious and not have any conscious idea why.

Conversely, if what I brought into the coffee bar with me was that I am appreciated and have value, and that people are essentially good, our discussion about the weather will activate that internal system as well. The underlying beliefs about my relationships with self, other, and the world will teach all these friendly notions by expanding the conversation a little, somehow legitimately wishing you, a good human being, a good day. This could be communicated by maintaining eye contact, having a friendly tone, and in the end perhaps offering you my name. As you walk away, you might feel a little better about your day and you also might not know why.

Both of these possibilities exist when having the same conversation about the same weather with the same two people. The question is not whether I am communicating or impacting those around me; the question is, what am I communicating, and therefore how am I impacting those around me? The implications of this are profound. Your world, and the world as we know it, is a result of what we are all inputting or uploading into these channels, the lines of communication in our web of connection.

If you are like most people, you probably believe that you are not transmitting these destructive underlying relationship messages. If you are like most people, you may be puzzled about why your world has arranged itself in a less-than-ideal way. If you are like most people, you are confused about why you feel the way you do. That is because, like most people, you aren't aware of what is going on in your basement.

THE BASEMENT: IT ALL STARTED IN RELATIONSHIP

The difficulties we experience in life, which are ultimately relationship difficulties, are because of what we hold in the basement of our psyches. If our psyche is metaphorically a house, the basement is the place where we hide our fears and vulnerabilities. We all have fears in the basement about not being good enough, being inadequate, unlovable, and so on, but we rarely reveal these fears. Instead, we hide, pretend, and defend, and that is ultimately what gets us into trouble.

> If our psyche is metaphorically a house, the basement is the place where we hide our fears and vulnerabilities.

In order to fully understand how this works, we have to take you through your developmental process. You are born into a particular family system, a particular web of relationships. In this system, people have experienced losses and challenges and have developed ways to deal with these losses. Your family has a history and a way of being that predates your entry into it.

Your journey begins in utero. The first part of your brain to develop, in the second trimester, is your brain stem, commonly known as your "reptilian" brain. This is your survival, flight-or-fight, instinctual level of being. It is fear-based. There you are, floating around happily in the womb, and already you are influenced by your family system: if your parent is feeling anxiety, you also feel that anxiety. You don't have the ability to interpret it, but chemically you will become used to a certain degree of anxiety, depending on what is happening in your family relationships at the time. You start to develop a "thermostat" for what feels familiar. Not necessarily what feels good, but what feels familiar.

Our emotional brain (cortex and limbic system) gets wired up in the six months or so after birth as part of the bonding process with our caregivers. We are wired for love and connection before anything else, which we believe has a spiritual as well as a survival-based reason for being. We are wired to feel love and connection before we are wired to think. On a spiritual level, we enter this world set up to wrestle with the duality of fear and love. On a human level, infants are highly vulnerable, and so the loving bond we form with our caregivers facilitates survival.

We operate primarily from our emotions all through our

childhoods. Our thinking brain, or neocortex, starts to kick in at around age five (usually when sequential memory begins) and isn't fully developed until early adulthood. As children, we are emotional beings driven by connection first and thinking beings able to sort facts and understand nuances second. Connection continues to be vitally important throughout our lives, despite most adults preferring to insulate themselves from this reality by dulling their feelings. Adults who feel connected live longer, happier, healthier lives.

We are born into a system, often to well-intentioned and imperfect parents who were raised by well-intentioned and imperfect parents. At some point in time, something painful happens, often with the people who love us, and this "happening" lays the foundation for all the difficulties we end up having in relationships with others. We develop a basement in our psyches, which exists at an emotional rather than an intellectual level (because our primary operating system is emotional).

Sometimes something overtly traumatic happens, like being hit, yelled at, or abused in some way. Sometimes something covertly traumatic happens, typically when part of our being is invalidated or ignored. In other instances, it might just be when rules of conduct are enforced, such as when a parent might perpetually instruct a child to never do anything risky, stemming from a loss in the family system when someone may have been seriously injured or handicapped from an accident.

If it feels like the bond we have with an important other (like a caregiver) is threatened, that invokes intense fear, because we instinctively believe we need to maintain that bond to survive. Whenever a child is faced with a perceived choice to be who they are or maintain the bond with the important other (by maintaining their love and approval), they will always choose to sacrifice self to maintain the bond, because it is experienced as a survival-based choice. "I am not allowed to be angry, it is bad to be angry, I am bad…" In this way we sentence part of ourselves to the basement, to be hidden and locked away.

> Whenever a child is faced with a perceived choice to be who they are or maintain the bond with the important other (by maintaining their love and approval), they will always choose to sacrifice self to maintain the bond, because it is experienced as a survival-based choice.

What happens in this moment of terror is that we literally start to feel that who we are is flawed, not good enough, unlovable. In those moments, we are flooded with fear and shame, and we think, "Oh no…what have I done?" We experience fear, guilt, and shame, and believe we must be bad, wrong, flawed, unworthy, and variations on that theme. We take on what we call a "suspicion of self," SOS for short. Though we seem here to be describing a thought, this suspicion of self is actually more of a feeling (shame) that hides a thought ("not good enough").

This is important to understand, because it is the feeling we put in the basement, and in these painful moments we learn to separate thinking from feeling. We have a certain intellectual understanding of who we are and how we operate, which differs from how we feel. This is the dilemma facing most adults: we know better intellectually (after all, we have our "shelf help" section at home to refer to), and what we know doesn't match how we feel. We end up in a constant inner argument between what we know to be true and how we feel, trying to talk ourselves out of our feelings.

Suspicion of self: SOS from the basement

Catherine:

I have struggled with several different things in my basement, one centred around my relationship with my father. I grew up in a Christian-principled, loving family as the oldest with a younger brother. My dad was a Presbyterian minister who felt a strong personal calling to ease the suffering of others. Both my parents are active humanitarians who, in their late seventies and eighties, continue to work in a volunteer capacity to make a difference in their local and global community. I inherited my faith in the importance of loving action from them: I attempt to make the world a better place every day through caring for others, as do my parents. My mother was the primary caregiver in our household and was the one my brother and I would turn to first if we needed help and support.

My father ended up leaving his position as a minister for social work, although both my parents remained very actively involved in the church. When I was young, my dad was very focused on his work, which was a mission for him. At one point he was travelling to Native reservations in remote Northern Ontario for his position with Probation and Parole. He was deeply impacted by the plight of the Natives living on these poverty-stricken reserves. He didn't see himself as an enforcer in this role; he saw himself as a counsellor. He cared a great deal for the people he had under his wing, and brought his work home with him emotionally; he would sometimes receive phone calls late at night from one of his clients calling for help. He was often stressed, and suffered from migraine headaches.

If I wanted my father's time or attention at the wrong moment, or if I had transgressed in some way, he could really lose his temper. He didn't get violent, but he got very loud and scary. These moments seemed unpredictable, as they were attached to a small trigger of some kind—some small thing around the house that my brother or I had not done, for example—and happened in the context of what was normally a very nice, polite home atmosphere. As this became a theme in our household, my mother would intervene or try to steer me or my brother away from my father when he was obviously stressed. There were also times when family events were cancelled, rearranged, or interrupted because of his work.

My mother was the glue in our family. When my dad lost his temper, she would pull him aside and talk to him. He would often come into our rooms to apologize afterwards. My mom reminds me that she also yelled at times, but I don't remember that in quite the same way, likely because the attachment I had to her was strong; and certainly she didn't lose her temper as often or as loudly.

What I experienced with my dad was more a theme than a single traumatic moment. He was away a lot, at one point up to three weeks of each month, and when he was home his attention was pulled elsewhere, either with work or with the church, where he remained intensely involved. This, along with his occasional explosions, coalesced into an SOS of "I am not important, I am a problem" in my basement.

I also wrestled with friendships as a young girl. I grew up in a small town where circles of friendship stayed pretty stable right through high school. Particularly in elementary school, I could never find my way into a group of friends. I would be "in" for a short while; then I would be "out," and I would never understand what had happened. I had one more-consistent friend, who I called my best friend, but who eventually "broke up" with me in Grade 4. "Not good enough" was this theme.

Perhaps a more obvious traumatic event occurred when I was eight or nine. I was on a sleepover at my best friend's home. She was the youngest of five: she had an older sister and three older brothers, two still living at home. Her parents had emigrated from Liverpool,

UK, and her home was very different than mine; in retrospect, I would say both her parents were alcoholics. Yelling occurred in her home on a regular basis, including between her parents. (I never saw mine argue.)

My best friend shared a room with her sister, who was away at a sleepover herself. I slept in the top bunk and my friend had the bottom. I woke up in the middle of the night hearing breathing close to me, and I realized that one of the brothers was standing over my bed. The room was dark.

When we feel threatened, we have three instinctive responses: fight, flight, or freeze. In that moment, I froze. He peeled back the covers, lifted up my nightie, and proceeded to sexually molest me. The whole time, I kept my eyes closed and pretended to be asleep. I dissociated, which means essentially removing self from the physical experience of what happened. Even today I don't recall much of how this felt: I have a strong sense of the room, of his breathing and position over the bed, but not of what was happening in my body. He eventually left, and I got a brief glimpse of him from the light in the hallway as he opened and closed the door. He was wearing a striped T-shirt, but he was mostly in shadow.

The next day, when my friend and I were walking home, I told her what happened. "Don't tell your dad!" she said. "My brother will get into so much trouble!" She then asked me which brother (of the two possibilities) it was. I didn't know. She asked a few questions, ending with "Was he big or little?" I told her he was big, because to me he was big.

I later learned that my friend had gone to her parents and told them what had happened. The oldest brother, who would have been maybe 16 at the time, was kicked out of the home and was not welcome there anymore. The next time I was over at my friend's house having lunch, the younger brother (who would have been 14 or so) walked into the kitchen...wearing the same red and white striped T-shirt I had briefly glimpsed in the hallway light as he was leaving the room. He kind of smirked at me.

I was horrified. I don't remember saying anything to anyone about this, but for many years the guilt over identifying the wrong brother overrode the trauma of being sexually molested for me. My suspicion of self was that I was a horrible, bad, dangerous person. I remember many years later, when I was seventeen, being swamped with the same horror when my dad mentioned in passing at the dinner table that the oldest brother of this family, the one I had mistakenly identified as the perpetrator, was in Stony Mountain Penitentiary (a high-security prison).

I never did tell my parents (until later in adulthood), and in retrospect, I believe part of the reason was because this friend was probably the only reliable friend I had at the time. Having her subsequently break up with me on the schoolyard was one of the more painful moments of my childhood. I did not connect the dots until years later, but this break-up happened not too long after the incident with her brother. I do remember her telling me in that conversation that she belonged in the "bad" crowd rather than with me.

Duane:

I am a male with three sisters, who grew up in a home whose emotional climate was characterized by a classic binge-drinking Irish alcoholic father. Paddy, as a sober father, had many wonderful attributes, including great humour, wit, audacity, and compassion. He had a huge heart. Much of what I hold in my skills and talents I would attribute to him.

However, when Paddy drank and returned home from the pub, he would declare war on my mother, Lorraine, for ruining his life. She was 15 when she met my father, who was 22. Shortly after, my mother became pregnant with my older sister, Claire. My father had an ambition at the time to become a professional baseball player. This sort of dream certainly would not have been commonplace in the farmlands of Northern Alberta (where they were both from), and thus a notable aspiration. His rage towards my mother for having to give up us his baseball career for marriage became the backdrop of anger I would have to endure.

Once every few weeks, he would wake the entire household, as well as the neighbourhood. He was physically and verbally violent, to the point where my mother would be weeping and begging for him to stop. My self-appointed role as an eight-year-old and beyond was to sequester my mother and my sisters to their rooms to minimize any emotional and physical damage. The horror and fear that I felt included the possibility that someone might actually die. Towards the end of these horrible nights, the effects of the alcohol on his system would eventually render him sitting sadly alone with his bottle. He would often continue to hold his party of one, singing drunken renditions of "Danny Boy," a popular song among Irish immigrants. This went on for years.

I was taken to the hospital on two occasions from defending my mother. The first occurred one night when my father ended up on top of me holding me to the ground. My sister Laverne came to my rescue, smashing his whiskey bottle over his head, with the broken glass severely cutting me just below the eye. There was so much blood, I could not see. Another evening, my father took out a rifle and was threatening to kill my mother. I attempted to stop him by grabbing the rifle. He gave me the butt end to my face, resulting in a round of stitches to my lip.

On another occasion, my father put a bullet through the living room window. The SWAT squad showed up. I was terrified for the safety of my mother and my sisters, and equally that my father was going to be shot. They captured my father, Paddy, throwing him in the back of a police van. In perhaps the most poignant moment of my life, I can still hear my father calling out my name, helplessly handcuffed in the back of the van, pleading with me to help him. Despite the pain we were all in, I loved my father. I knew he loved me, and I felt enormous sadness, compassion, and guilt for not protecting him as well. I felt his pain. It may be the only time I heard my father actually ask for help.

For the most part, I successfully kept the knowledge of my home life separate from my world of friends and school. I attended St. Mary's Elementary Catholic school in Vancouver's East End. Students attending Catholic school would live miles from each other, unlike those in the public school system. This served me well in keeping the secret of my house of horrors from the outside world. I was an altar boy as well, hoping that somehow serving on the altar and being closer to God would allow me a privileged status for the doling out of any miracles coming from heaven. I was active athletically, well liked, and extremely popular. It was important to me to keep it that way.

As an 11-year-old, I invited my good friend Ronnie, a fellow altar boy, to my home for a Friday overnight, with the promise of playing Monopoly, PJs, popcorn, and oatmeal with brown sugar and cartoons in the morning. This was a risk, as it was also payday. Payday meant cash in the pocket and some extended time in the pub. Six p.m. came with dinner and no Paddy. Eight p.m. and still no sight of him. If he wasn't home by then, chances were he had moved from the pub and beer to someone's home and the hard stuff. The hard stuff would bring out the worst in him. It went on like this until we fell asleep close to midnight. Terrified, I heard Paddy's steps coming up the front stairwell. From my downstairs bedroom, I could tell by the way he walked up those stairs what he'd drunk, how much he'd drunk, and what was about to happen. It wasn't good.

He entered our house with a couple of drinking buddies in tow to continue his drinking binge. This was accompanied by loud and aggressive cursing, bodies falling on the floor, and ashtrays smashing against the wall. I was scared. Nights like this were commonplace, and tonight was certainly no exception. Normally, I would run as quickly as possible to usher my mother and sisters into their bedrooms and stand on guard while trembling inside.

Ronnie bolted up out of bed, having never witnessed anything like this. Ronnie came from a "good" family, with attentive parents and a safe and caring family life. It was January and a particularly cold January for Vancouver. Ice on the roads. Ronnie lived two miles away. He ran out of the house barefoot, crying for his parents, and I took chase. What would I have done if I'd caught up to him? Bring him back to…what? After a block, I let Ronnie run home and collapsed on the frozen ground on hands and knees. I had nowhere to go. I returned home to take care of my mother and sisters, but hurting terribly and now extremely anxious that I had lost my best friend.

My two worlds were now in collision. I'd been found out. I feared my life was over as I knew it. If there had been an ongoing trial concerning my worth, my value, or who I intrinsically was, it had now reached its verdict. Guilty, flawed, defective, not good enough as charged! I hid these feelings in my basement, believing I was a miserable excuse for a person. Despite my depth of pain, I felt for my father's as well.

Monday morning at school, Ronnie, thankfully, remained my supportive friend. I was truly grateful for his heart.

Through these early years of our development, connection and survival are interchangeable, so whenever there appears to be a choice between being our real selves or preserving connection, we will always choose connection over authenticity. We relegate what we believe to be the shameful aspect of ourselves to the basement of our psychological house, where we lock it up and preferably throw away the key. Sadly, in so doing we also throw away part of ourselves.

We have heard some pretty horrific stories of things that happened to people as children in our work. However, even without the obviously traumatic events that many of us do experience, it is impossible to get out of childhood without developing a basement to some degree. This isn't because of bad parenting, it is simply because of how we develop as human beings: we do not have the ability to understand nuances and context until adulthood. If we accept this, then we can proceed with the task of adulthood, reclaiming self from the basement in an integrated fashion, so what we know to be true matches what we feel to be true. That is what we can do to prevent the horrific stories from replaying in the next generation.

STRATEGIC SELF DEVELOPS TO COMPENSATE FOR OUR SUSPICION OF SELF

These moments are intensely painful for a child. Metaphorically, it is as if we cut off aspects of our authentic self through these experiences in order to preserve connection, particularly with our caregivers. We take on these suspicions about self in these traumatic moments of shame, fear, and horror, believing that who we are isn't good enough, is unlovable, shameful, and flawed.

We create a defence system in the very moment our SOS is birthed. The next question that occurs to us as soon as we fear that we are not good enough is "What do I have to do to get the love back? How will I survive, now that I am flawed?" We try behaviour A; it doesn't work. Behaviour B; it doesn't work. Behaviour C…it works! I have the love and approval of my caregivers.

In that moment, we decide "Who I am isn't good enough to be loved; I will become Behaviour C." We develop a strategic self, initially a mask on the porch to our house, in order to cover up what we fear about ourselves in the basement of our psyches. This strategic self replaces who we fear we are (SOS) with who we have surmised we need to be (mask) in order be viewed as an acceptable person. We fear that we are flawed, when in reality we are anything but. We hide our apparent flaws behind masks and strategies.

Catherine:

The Behaviour C that I landed on, both with my dad and with "friends," was to learn to read the expectations of others and put their needs ahead of my own. I can remember on summer holidays while school was out spending hours imagining the new and improved person I would become when school started again in the fall. I became a "pleaser," constantly adjusting to what was wanted from me rather than putting forward what I wanted myself. I learned to read my dad's facial expression, particularly the vein in his forehead that would become prominent as his stress levels rose. I would then back off and adjust so that I could avoid the blow-up. At least, that was my strategy until I hit my teens, when I became far more concerned about pleasing my boyfriend than about pleasing my father! We call this "overfunctioning" in relationships.

I decided to compensate for the horror of making a mistake in the only logical way: I decided I would never make a mistake. I became a perfectionist.

Duane:

My strategic self, or my Behaviour C, was to become Superboy. I would become the answer to the Antichrist father. I was an altar boy—head altar boy, in fact. I was the saviour of women. This was my identity on the porch. I came from a large family of Catholics on both sides; the mothers and aunts would travel far and wide to sit in St. Mary's Church adoring the cute, innocent lad in his starched and ironed altar boy tunic and cassock serving Mass. "He is such a good boy, unlike his father," I would hear them say. I was the second coming in our family system. I was equally hero to my father's villain—all the while using my facade on the porch as a means of having one-way relationships, in order to ensure that no one entered my home and uncovered the SOS I was holding hostage in the basement of my psyche. I hated who I was down there. I had no idea the problems this answer to my problems would create for me down the road in my life.

Now, the problem is that instead of repairing these false notions about the self that we hide in the basement of our psyches, we concentrate our time and personality development on inventing more sophisticated strategies on the porch. The strategic self amplifies and develops as we grow, while the aspect of our real self that we have cut off (SOS) remains emotionally frozen in time. We continue to encounter difficult and predictable life events, and we continue to develop our strategic self to make up for our fears about who we are in the basement. Who we fear we are in the basement stays where we left it—not going away but growing in power with our fear of it.

Sadly, this SOS, this lie about who we have decided we must be in that dark corner of our basement, remains perceived as a truth, in fact, an ultimate truth. If we believe the painful experiences we encountered as children were solely responsible for the damaging impact on our sense of self and happiness, that can't hold a candle to what we have done to ourselves since. We sentence part of ourselves to the basement of our psyche with the intention that this aspect of who we fear we are will never be seen again or noticed. In fact, this self-inflicted mental cruelty is where the real crime and damage occurs.

The basement is only a basement because we hide what we fear about our real self by covering it with a strategic self.

The basement is only a basement because we hide what we fear about our real self by covering it with a strategic self.

THE TWO LAYERS OF THE STRATEGIC SELF: MASK AND ARMOUR

Our strategic self has two layers to it. One is our mask, whose purpose is to make up for and distract both ourselves and others from our SOS (hidden in the basement). Our mask can present as a saviour, a nice person, a giver, a comic, a workaholic, a pleaser, a perfectionist, a chameleon, a doormat, invisible, the life of the party, a performer, an intellectual, a jellyfish with no boundaries, a liar, co-dependent or needy, a wounded bird, or a runner. These are a few of the character facades we use to strategically present ourselves in the hopes of getting a certain positive outcome. We figure out what works in our families of origin through trial and error, but these same strategies certainly won't work later on in life, as we shall see.

The mask or facade, however, is not the only tool in our toolkit. It is important to remember that these masks have a hidden agenda: the goal of Behaviour C is to "get the love back." We don the mask with the goal of having our strategies work, aiming to achieve something or please someone. We seek something outside ourselves (the right partner, education, income level, etc.) to make up for our fears about ourselves in the basement. When the mask doesn't work, when the reward isn't forthcoming, we bring out our armour: the unique attack strategies we also learned in our family of origin.

For example, for some the strategy of doing all for everyone, giving and giving, has a secret mission: to get approval. These "givers" are trusting that if they are needed and make themselves necessary, then they will be valued and eventually given to. When this strategy fails (and it will), their war cry becomes "I give, I give, and I give. Why don't I ever get?" From the armour beneath the giver mask, they may become passive-aggressive, with silent upset and perhaps eventually explosive anger, punishing the one who was supposed to deliver for not coming through with their part of the under-the-table deal. The mask donned is one of a perpetual and committed giver, and the weapon concealed beneath and ready for action is the withholder. Most of us can be nice, until we aren't. Cooperative until we are resentful. Flattering until we are frustrated.

Of course, some of these strategic mask personality constructions are also positive attributes. The question to ponder is more about what is driving these behaviours. When and what for? For example, driven by anxiety and the SOS, the overfunctioner will try to get something to make up for what they fear they are. In a less anxious situation, while feeling good and close, giving to another may be simply a well-developed and compassionate action. These behaviours or actions can be our best strength or our worst weakness—an attribute or a problem, depending on what is driving them.

When these masks fail, others then encounter our armour. We attack and blame, with weapons as unique as the tools we have developed at a mask level. Ultimately, our armour is constructed for the same purpose as the mask: to protect what we have hidden in the basement. What is really happening as we wander obliviously through our daily lives is that something or someone triggers our underlying suspicion of self and we don our armour to protect ourselves, attacking the thing that triggered our old, historic fear. We mistake the person knocking on the door to the basement for the one who put us there. However, that isn't how it feels; it feels as if him or her or this or that is causing our upset rather than simply triggering it.

For all of us, there are two important goals to achieve with the construction of this strategic self. The first is that the person we are developing a strategic self for behaves accordingly and plays by our rules, or provides us in kind with what we believe we need to make up for what we fear we are. The second part of the deal is that we keep the person far away from the person we fear we are in the basement. We fear that if we let that aspect of self be revealed, we will be rejected. To prevent that outcome, we consciously or unconsciously do what it takes to push people away when they try to enter.

In the end, then, no matter how successful these strategies are in attracting or controlling the one or many you are directing these actions towards for some outcome, these people will never be allowed into your house because of what you fear they might find in your basement. It is in the basement that attention is required and, ironically, the only place it is not allowed.

What we are hiding in the basement is at the root of the problem. Because we fear we are unlovable, guilty, not good enough, and so on, we position ourselves in a certain way in our relationships, sending messages of fear through our unique relationship web. We hide, pretend, and defend. We think this is going to work for us, but it actually works against us.

SELF-APPLICATION

Hopefully our stories have helped you to reflect on your own. Some people easily relate to the idea of having a suspicion of self, a fear that they are flawed, not good enough, unlovable, and so on. If you are one of these people, where did you make this up initially? What happened that put you in the basement? Others have become more identified with their strategic self and are less aware of what might be hiding and impacting them in their basement. If you are among this group, consider some of the events of your childhood and imagine those same events happening to others (your children, for example, if you have any). Sometimes it is easier to see the impact if we imagine events happening to others, particularly those we love.

1. Journal about this event as if it were a newspaper article. Put your suspicion of self as the headline, e.g., "Catherine Is Unlovable," "Duane Is Flawed, Just Like Dad," and then write a few short paragraphs about the event itself. Take your time with this, and be gentle with yourself.
2. What masks or strategies do you use to hide your SOS in the basement (the newspaper headline)?

2 Problems Are Reinforced in Relationships (The Present)

It is not the end of the physical body that should worry us. Rather, our concern must be to live while we're alive—to release our inner selves from the spiritual death that comes with living behind a facade designed to conform to external definitions of who and what we are.

—Dr. Elizabeth Kübler-Ross

There is more to who we are than our suspicion of self (SOS), of course; however, it is our SOS that is at the root of so many of the dilemmas we face in life. These fear-based beliefs about self were born in a moment of disconnection. They happened in relationship to another human being. Now there is a part of us (not the whole of us) sentenced to the basement of our psyche, where we fear we are unlovable, not good enough, flawed. There is now an aspect we hold separate and hidden in the basement, and instead our strategic self engages with the world.

We stop being real. We stop taking risks. This part of us

sits on the sidelines, waiting for life to magically happen, rather than entering the playing field. We aren't necessarily aware of how much we contribute to our own dilemmas in this way.

When we run into difficulty in our relationships, we think of the problem as being either inside self or inside the other. More often than not, if we are honest, we think of problems as being inside the other. For example, couples coming in for counselling are often secretly (or not so secretly) hoping that we will just fix their partner, since they are obviously the problem!

As we have seen, however, we aren't individuals, we are individuals-in-constant-connection. Everything we think, feel, say, or do has influence on others, and we are also constantly being influenced by those around us. We can only ever truly understand ourselves in the context of the relationship landscape that surrounds us, our relationship web. The connecting lines in our relationship web are active: we are constantly downloading, uploading, and passing along emotional information, both positive and negative, helpful and harmful.

Despite having SOSs hidden in the basement of our psyche, the problems we face in life are kept alive through our relationship dynamics in all the lines of our web. That is where they get refueled. How we hide, pretend, defend, and offend in all our relationships is key to what we end up experiencing.

DEFENCES CREATE WHAT THEY DEFEND AGAINST

All our well-intentioned strategies and less well-intentioned defences and armour are destined to backfire and result in the very experience we are trying to avoid. How we hide, pretend, defend, and offend sends fearful messages through the circuits of our relationship web, which return to us. This is the ultimate irony of the whole complex system. Despite our feeling justified in reacting with what seems to be a logical defence, our strategy doesn't work and, in fact, creates the very thing we are defending against.

There is a clever yogic saying: "Being angry is like taking poison and expecting the other person to die." It is perhaps apparent that when you explode in anger, you never feel better. When a discussion erupts into an angry fight, you might have a moment of "I told them!" righteousness, but it doesn't take long until you begin to revisit what you said and feel guilty about it. The guilt you feel about this defended action quickly translates into shame: "What kind of horrible person am I?" Your own actions reinforce your underlying suspicion of self.

Catherine:

Many of us, myself included, prefer to practise the fine art of passive aggression (instead of overt aggression). I learned both models in my family of origin, so both exist in my toolkit, but the one I am more apt to pull out is the less messy one. Rather than fighting Duane, I practise the skills of emotional responsibility, but early in our relationship we were far less capable.

Duane would do something that upset me. In response, I would silently broadcast my displeasure, permeating the entire atmosphere with my cold disapproval and sucking anything positive from the environment. If he were so bold as to ask, "Is there anything wrong?" I would of course reply, "No, I am fine…," because the purpose of the exercise was to get him to engage in a ruthless self-inventory to discover for himself what he'd done wrong. Needless to say, this dishonest and defended approach never worked particularly well, and in fact caused tremendous suffering for both of us. We both felt miserable.

Duane:

Superman, my tried-and-true mask, can save, of course, but he can also fly away, and he knows how to fight. If I felt my strategies for managing a safe distance and, at the same time, receiving adoration failed—if I was greeted with Catherine's (or any woman's) attempts to become closer to me, or, once closer, criticize me in any way—Superman could start acting more like Darth Vader. The emotional climate of my family certainly trained me in the not-so-fine art of emotional guerilla warfare. Depending on the level of anxiety, my defences included cutting humour, diagnosing the other as the problem, or all-out yelling and threatening to leave. All of this transmitted the aggressive theme of rejecting the other where the other was vulnerable and hurting.

The promise of this defence would be that the other would see the error of her ways and return to adoring me and, at the same time, allow enough distance to secure safety. This never happened. In my attempts to essentially find my innocence by making another guilty, I was met with more criticism, upset, and hostility. The personal hell I was defending against would only come back to me like an avalanche. With Catherine, I would give her every reason to be more distant, critical, and fearful of me. All adding up to the very opposite outcome of what I apparently wanted. Or was it?

It is less obvious that our well-intentioned strategies (Behaviour C) are equally destined to backfire. This is true whether they actually work (meaning we achieve what we wanted) or whether they don't. Let's take a popular relationship strategy—overfunctioning—as an example. Overfunctioning means that you take care of far more than your share of a relationship. One way of doing so is the giver mask we referred to in the last chapter.

If every relationship adds up to 100%, a healthy relationship stance is when you practise 100% of your 50%—no more and no less. When you practise more, you are overfunctioning; when you practise less, you are underfunctioning. This applies both to the nuts-and-bolts concrete tasks of a home or workplace and to the psychological and emotional life of any relationship. A client in a relationship with an overfunctioner once described this dynamic beautifully: "It is like we are playing tennis," he said, "and she hits the ball to me, then runs to my side of the net and hits it back to herself!"

You are overfunctioning when you psychically occupy another person's being and probe for what they are thinking or feeling in an effort to be "helpful." You are doing for them what they can do, or must learn to do, for themselves.

Overfunctioning is often applauded because it can appear to be a loving act. Overfunctioners give (and give and give). But if we take a closer look, we can see that this isn't actually true. Doing more than your 50% requires someone else to be doing less than theirs: someone must leave a gap for the overfunctioner to fill.

Overfunctioning tends to be a strategy learned by someone trying to make up for a fear of not being good enough (in the basement). If I am afraid at an emotional level that I am not good enough, I will overdo to prove my worth and my value. I will need to be needed. I will set up my world to make sure that I am needed.

The cry of the overfunctioner is this: "How come no one ever considers me?"

The answer is, because you train them not to. You have set up contracts in your relationship web that state you will do more than your 50%, and the people in your life adjust to doing less in response. This isn't a lack of appreciation; this is how the relationship system has to adjust to what you have put into it. If they tried to do their 50%, they would literally have to push you (at 80%) out of the way.

Overfunctioners end up not being considered, which reinforces their suspicion that they aren't good enough or worthy of being considered. If the overfunctioner isn't able to consider self or love self, the sad reality is that no one else can either. How can another consider you if you do not? How can someone love you where you don't? There would be nowhere for that consideration or love from another to be filed, at best, or even noticed, at worst.

Sarah was the oldest of three siblings. Sarah had a close relationship with her mother, who was an attentive caregiver, until Sarah reached the age of four. At that point, she had one younger brother. When Sarah was four, her parents' marriage hit a crisis point when Mom discovered Dad had cheated on her multiple times. Mom packed up the kids and moved back in with her parents for a little over two years.

During that year, not only was Mom's (and Dad's) attention diverted from their children because of the crisis in their marriage, Mom also had to return to work full time to support herself and the children. The two children saw their father but lived with Mom and her parents. Dad and Mom frequently fought.

The dynamic in Mom's family of origin was difficult, as her father was a patriarchal tyrant who ruled the household with an iron fist. Sarah was cared for physically by her grandmother but frequently found herself stepping in to protect her young brother from her critical, controlling grandfather. Sarah felt the loss of her mother profoundly at this young age, and as children do, held that this was somehow all her fault and that she was not good enough in some way.

Mom and Dad eventually got back together, but that didn't

have a happy ending for Sarah. They very quickly had a new child, a daughter, and Sarah felt replaced by this younger and cuter girl. She continued to feel on the outside, and the strategy she employed to find her way in was to become a deputy parent. She learned to overfunction. Her overfunctioning served her well career-wise, as she became a well-respected director of services for various care facilities.

Sarah sought counselling at the age of forty because she wanted help to know "what to do" about her relationship with her mother. She was by now married with two children of her own, and was upset at the apparent lack of care her mother had for her. Her mother would frequently cancel lunch dates or change childcare arrangements at the last minute. She would talk to Sarah about her grandchildren but not ask about Sarah herself. Once again, Sarah felt on the outside.

Sarah had decided that her mother was unreliable, and so had for the most part stopped making plans with her that that didn't have flexibility. Sarah's mother did call her for advice and help with family issues, which Sarah provided. Sarah continued in the role she had learned at the age of five: even though she might complain when Mom had to cancel on her, she continued to act as deputy parent.

Sarah came to the session armed with notes, notebook, and pen. She didn't want to forget any of the directives that might be provided to her. She was upset because she felt she had tried many different things with her mother, most of which involved informing Mom of what she needed as a daughter, and none had worked to date.

Like all overfunctioners, Sarah's busyness had a hidden agenda: it allowed her to focus on "what to do" and avoid what she was feeling. Sarah had a tremendous amount of pain and vulnerability that she was unwilling to acknowledge and certainly didn't know how to communicate. Instead of allowing herself to feel her sadness, which is an important therapeutic first step, she spent her time coming up with solutions to fix the problem. Her strategy of providing Mom with directives only served to increase the distance between them rather than invite connection.

"The caretaker and the wounded bird" is a variation on the over- and underfunctioner relationship dynamic. The caretaker, despite cheerleading the wounded bird's recovery, will unconsciously train the wounded bird not to mend his or her wounds. This is mostly due to the wounded one never being left alone long enough to take care of self or have an opportunity to learn how. There is a difference between caretaking and caring for, which we will get to later. This is a difference the caretaker is ignorant of. The underfunctioner becomes more and more underfunctioning as the overfunctioner becomes more and more overfunctioning. The cycle not only continues but feeds itself in an endless loop. Sometimes, in addictions circles particularly, this is referred to as "enabling." All of these come under the overfunctioning umbrella.

Part of what keeps the cycle going is that the overfunctioner cannot sit in their anxiety long enough to actually allow the underfunctioner to feel the weight of their dilemma and step up. The problem becomes what the one is triggering in the other: the anxiety beneath and fueling this behaviour is the overfunctioner's SOS—a variation of "I am not enough." For example, if a parent notices a child leaving a mess and makes that mess mean that the parent is a bad parent (SOS), the parent cannot stand the anxiety of this SOS very long and, rather than wait for the child to clean up the mess, the parent will clean it up and complain about the irresponsible child. This behaviour is being driven by not only a desire to clean up a mess, but more so to shut down the upset in the basement. The child learns to rely on the parent cleaning the mess up. Behind the scenes, the defence system has re-identified the problem from the fear of being a bad parent to having a bad child. The child learns how to live up to that reputation.

The same dynamic is true in adult relationships. These postures and positions—these strategic selves—make agreements unconsciously together, all in an attempt to sidestep the anxiety inside the basement both ways. The overfunctioning adult can see the problem as being the other person's, and thus justify continuing to caretake and adapt the situation so that the underfunctioner never has to deal with their own problems. This is akin to a goaltender in a soccer match facing an opponent who takes a shot and misses the target badly: the overfunctioner metaphorically moves the goalposts in order for the unskilled player to score.

The underfunctioner has an equal and opposite strategy, founded on a similar fear of not being good enough. Instead of trying to prove their worth, they decide to avoid making mistakes or potentially getting into trouble. They avoid and distance themselves in relationships and, at the extreme, also cut off (meaning that they leave, or decide not to speak to someone anymore). Underfunctioners fear failure and, as a result, abdicate control to the overfunctioner, whom they can then blame (although not necessarily out loud) if things don't work out. A constant underlying sense of inadequacy is apparently avoided by refusing to enter territory where this feeling is activated. Just as in all strategies, however, underfunctioning also backfires, as these avoidant actions end up just reinforcing this sense of inadequacy and fear of failure.

The overfunctioner and the underfunctioner have entered into an unconscious agreement and vicious circle of reinforcing the very thing they are both trying to get rid of. These two can easily remain in a dysfunctional relationship, complaining about each other, all the while feeling safer because the battleground is perceived in the relationship now, instead of in the self.

ACTING OUT AND ACTING IN

Our strategic and defended actions (Behaviour Cs, such as over- and underfunctioning) may be categorized into "acting out" and "acting in" behaviours. These are positions we adopt as a means of making up for our SOS in the basement. Sometimes we do so by withdrawing and pulling away in relationship (acting in), holding the anxiety and fear within and attempting to deal with it internally. Sometimes we do so by actively inputting into a relationship (acting out), feeling the anxiety and fear and attempting to fix, manipulate, or control it "out there," in another person. Below are some examples of acting-out and acting-in relationship behaviours.

Acting out behaviours include:
- Overfunctioning: caretaking, perfecting/performing/ pleasing/approval-seeking, enabling, controlling
- Aggression: fighting, threats, violence, passive aggression
- Triangling: gossip, affairs
- Addictions: sex, gambling, shopping

Triangling requires a bit more explanation, because it is a go-to behaviour for so many of us. Triangling means that you deal with a problem or anxiety in one relationship by going to a third person and bringing your anxiety there instead. Typically, this means going to your best friend and achieving temporary relief by talking about it (and even better if you get agreement on your position!). Coffee shops are so successful because everyone is talking about someone who isn't there. Our best friends tend to be those who agree with us about whom we blame our emotional state on.

Affairs are an extreme form of triangling. One of the most hurtful aspects of some kinds of affairs is that the affair partner is the intimate partner—the one who knows more about what is going on in the betrayer's primary relationship, and what that person is thinking and feeling, than the primary relationship partner. Note that we are defining "affairs" here as a violation of a relationship agreement. If you have agreed to a non-monogamous relationship, we would not consider that to be an affair, obviously; but in our experience, triangling can be a major anxiety-binding aspect of polyamorous relationships.

The difficulty with triangling is that the problem is never resolved in the relationship where it exists. Triangling keeps the dilemma alive; it doesn't resolve it. We have observed some fairly ineffective therapy that qualifies as triangling, where a client comes week after week (sometimes for years) to vent about an issue and leaves feeling relieved but not resolved to do anything differently or see anything differently.

All of these are ways of acting out in a relationship system, and all will feed fear and anxiety into your relationship web, because all are founded on your underlying suspicion of self. Some of these overlap—for example, controlling can be both overfunctioning and aggressive. Affairs can be triangling and a sex addiction.

Acting in behaviours include:
- Underfunctioning: distancing, avoidance, cutting off, emotional cocooning
- Self-Aggression: depression, suicidal ideation, eating disorders

- Addictions: food or substance (which can escalate into acting out)
- Escape into fantasy: porn, TV, Internet

Recall that you cannot not communicate: an emotional cut-off is a powerful communication in a relationship, but you cannot actually disconnect by cutting off. Instead, when we cut off in a relationship we are sending a strong message into that relationship line or circuit: "I do not acknowledge your existence. I erase you." While we may achieve some temporary "out of sight, out of mind" relief by doing so, the next time we see that person or hear their name in conversation, all the feelings we were trying to avoid come right to the fore.

Frank, a 30-year-old client of ours, recently decided to visit his family in Toronto, Canada. He had been living in Vancouver for the past twenty years, mostly in an effort to get away from his family and start a new life here. After many sessions coaching him on hanging on to himself in the middle of a family that could be best characterized as reactive, blaming, and melodramatic, he was going back to spend Christmas at home.

His visit was planned to be two weeks, but after two days we received an email from him stating that he had seen the light and was going to leave. He went on to say that he could not relate to this group of fools—in his words—and had engaged in and benefitted from years of therapy. He claimed they were all backstabbing, irresponsible, and incapable of carrying on a real conversation. He was done and wanted our blessing to cut his visit short and our agreement that it was time to leave his family behind. We had one comment to make to him that changed his life forever.

We informed him that his way of leaving his family was his way of being in his family. What he was about to do, walking out the door, wasn't any different than what his family were doing battling inside those doors. If he were to leave, he would be conveying the same message from across the country as his family were conveying to each other screaming across the living room. He stayed.

Had he emotionally cut off communication and contact, Frank would have transmitted the same message to his family as they were to each other. Although the others were overt, arguing in the kitchen, he was no different in his covert leaving and cutting off communication; cutting off was his form of communication. Geographical location and time play no part in removing communication. The message being uploaded into the relationship lines was the same, and would have been maintained had he chosen to leave in judgment. Instead, he made a different choice.

"Emotional cocooning" requires a bit of explanation. Emotional cocooning occurs when you focus entirely on one relationship (usually a romantic one, or sometimes parent-child) and distance yourself in all other relationships. This can appear quite lovely, especially in our romance-worshipping society, but it creates a significant amount of pressure on one relationship. If something goes wrong in that one relationship, it has major repercussions.

A sad feature within the cocooning relationship, though rarely recognized, is that one member's quest to become an individual is perceived as a threat to the stability of the "we" and is undermined by the other; there is a high cost on having a "me" in the need for a "we." It requires a high level of maintenance to keep things going right in that one focused relationship. When cocooning happens in a parent-child relationship, it has major repercussions for the child, who isn't allowed to have anyone be more important than the parent.

(Note: The terms over- and underfunctioning [reciprocity], triangling, distance, cut-off, and emotional cocooning come from the Bowen family systems theory.)

THE ACTING OUT/IN CYCLE: OUR ATTEMPTS TO AVOID ANXIETY AMPLIFY IT

No one decides to become an alcoholic, be aggressive, or have an affair just for the fun of it. In fact, no one decides to seek approval or caretake for the fun of it either. All of these behaviours are driven by fear and anxiety. Very often the acting out/in behaviour that follows the fear trigger happens so quickly, we don't even notice that fear started the whole thing.

All of these are learned Behaviour Cs that appeared to work in the short term when we happened on them. The fear and anxiety comes from what we believe about ourselves in the basement (SOS). Something will happen in our relationship environment that will trigger our underlying suspicion of self, and we will feel fear, which is an automatic cue for our strategic behaviour to kick in.

The difficulty is that our actions are not neutral: they take place within a relationship system and have an impact on that system. This is true even if your Behaviour C is sitting alone watching endless TV. You are communicating your fear and distrust of the world through that action, and the message lands with somebody somewhere. It might be the person on the other end of a call you ignore, or the neighbour who always says hi with a big smile in the hallway and receives a cursory response.

Through these actions, we create contracts with the people around us. Our relationship web organizes itself around the unreal or strategic self that we put into it. Overfunctioners will have underfunctioners in their lives because without them they wouldn't be able to overfunction (until they collapse from exhaustion or illness and become underfunctioners themselves for a period of time).

Alcoholics and addicts will have enablers or caretakers. Aggressors need someone to fight with. Approval-seekers need someone who isn't easy to please, to make their efforts worthwhile. As long as we have pain locked up in the basements of our psyches, we will be seeking a way to explain that pain with him, her, this, or that.

> As long as we have pain locked up in the basement of our psyches, we will be seeking a way to explain that pain by him, her, this, or that.

In this way we set up the people around us to become the very thing we are trying to get away from in our past. Because of what we are hanging on to in our basement, we are wired for fear and defence. We are hyperalert for evidence that what happened back then is happening again. In essence, we see what we are looking for. It is as if those fear-based beliefs are written on the lenses of our glasses, and as we look through them we latch on to what agrees and screen out what doesn't.

Rather than perceiving the full breadth of reality in front of us, we prove our fears by focusing in this way on a small portion of what is in front of us. We are looking out through the lenses of our suspicion of self. We are hot-wired from the basement to react with our strategies and defences. How we respond then invites the very thing we are trying to avoid.

ATTACK AND BLAME IS PROJECTED GUILT AND SHAME

We end up seeing people a certain way because we are looking through the filters of our past, and because of how we see them, our behaviour makes sense. "This person is a _____, therefore

I must_____." If I am a man who believes women are going to emotionally castrate me (because I had an over-controlling mother, for example), I will behave badly to even the sweetest example of womankind, who is then likely to react badly to me. I will then walk away saying, "I told you so!"

Dan was a workshop client who had managed to alienate the entire female portion of our weekend workshop, at least 15 women, before the workshop even began. He was insulting, curt, and obnoxious; the women were ready to lynch him. There was a movement underway to eject him, as, understandably, the women did not feel safe with him in the room.

As the workshop began, after a period of time establishing agreements and safety, we interviewed Dan further. We eventually got underneath his armour to reveal what the guard was guarding: in this tender state, Dan confessed that he was an identical twin who had always been unfavourably compared to his older (by a few minutes) brother. He felt he could never please his critical mother, and eventually he just gave up. Underneath it all, he felt he was flawed, not good enough, and unlovable. He was tearful, curled up in a ball in his chair, head down.

We then asked the women where they wanted to be now, and they got up out of their chairs and moved to sit in front of him. They were drawn to his vulnerability, and there was caring and compassion in their eyes, which was everything Dan longed for. "Look up, Dan," we said. "Take a new picture." He was scared, and we spent some time encouraging him to question his own defence and take a vulnerable risk by letting himself receive the care that was present for him in the eyes of those sitting in front of him.

"No," he eventually said, with his head still down, looking at the ground in front of him. "They are only there because you told them to be." The women got up and moved back to their seats. Then Dan looked up and said, "See, I told you so!"

Now, Dan had a few better moments later on in the workshop, but this one is a tragic illustration of how the cycle works. We are not so much perceiving reality as projecting our own version of it, seeking to prove our own fear-based beliefs. Our defences create the very thing we are defending against. Our SOSs were made up in relationship with another person and must be corrected in connection with another person. We cannot heal alone.

All these acting out/in behaviours are meant to alleviate anxiety, and they do work, but only in a very temporary way. Addicts and alcoholics know this story well. They turn to the substance as a solution to the problem, but the solution amplifies the problem more and more over time, so they have to use the substance in ever-escalating quantities as their life erodes around them. All these behaviours work in a very similar way, in that they all end up amplifying our difficulty rather than alleviating it.

The dysfunctional behaviour springs from what we hold in our basements: the SOS and the strategy or defence linked to it. At the same time, you will not be fully aware of what is hiding in your basement if you continue with the behaviour. In fact, particularly with the behaviours that appear less destructive, you may not be aware at all of what is hiding in your basement because the twinge of anxiety triggers the cycle so quickly that you don't even notice what started it.

> In fact, particularly with the behaviours that appear less destructive, you may not be aware at all of what is hiding in your basement because the twinge of anxiety triggers the cycle so quickly that you don't even notice what started it.

The waves we create with what we upload into our

connecting relationship lines or system do not just go out. They return to us a perception of the world in front of us in such a way that it reinforces whatever we already believe about self, other, and the world.

As unlikely as this might be, imagine for a moment Charles Manson and Mother Teresa walking side by side through a ghetto in LA. Both have an identical experience in front of them: hungry and lost people living on the streets, engaging in criminal activity while abusing their bodies, each other, and substances and alcohol. The difference is they would have a fundamentally different type of activity being lit up in their 80% relationship message channels and the belief systems they brought along with them, and thus a different set of natural behaviours and relationship messages that they would extend.

Charles Manson would obviously demonstrate and communicate that the world is an unsafe place, bracing himself for danger, and defence would predictably become offence. He would be defiant and aggressive, believing those on the street to be defective and dangerous people who were sub-human and not worthy of his time, or he would choose to dominate them in some way. He would be uploading or injecting danger into those connecting lines, and danger would in turn come back to him in response to his projected view of those in front of him. Those on the street would pick up his aggressive challenge and respond accordingly. They might gang up on Charles. Charles might pull out a weapon, declaring, "See, I told you, Mother Teresa, no one is to be trusted and it was a good thing I was ready for those bastards."

Mother Teresa, on the other hand, is carrying with her an entirely different set of beliefs about self, other, and the world. She would communicate her belief in her own innocence by seeing the same thing in others. She would see the same street people, struggling with the same issues with crime and abuse, but would see these behaviours as a call for help or love. She would act accordingly, reaching out to them. It would be taught, felt, and their response would be perceived and experienced to be consistent with what she was believing.

Whatever the belief systems are that underpin our surface means of relating and posturing to the world, we will perceive only that which is necessary to staying where we already are and to what we already believe. A cynic will only see that which there is to remain cynical about. If love is all you truly want, love is all you will truly see. Whether it is fear or love, we only see and experience what we need to stay there. Both will call it reality.

We are 100% committed to the state we are in. It takes just as much work for Charles Manson to keep his insane citadel of defence, covering up and keeping his self-hatred alive, as it does for Mother Teresa to continue to see the innocence in self and others. It isn't a question of commitment. It is more a question of, what are we committed to?

We exist in a web, or system, of relationships. Within that system, we have an impact and are impacted. We are creatively uploading into our relationship-system circuitry what we believe about self and life, and what others mean to us, 24-7. The relationship system is also the context in which we grow and develop, the context in which we formulate our beliefs and learn how we have to behave, given what we believe.

THE STRATEGIC SELF KEEPS EVERYTHING OUT

The strategic self (including our masks, strategies, and armour) evolved to hide our suspicion of self in the basement of our psyche. We evolved all our defences and strategies in order to "get the love back," to do what we needed to do to survive in this world. The irony is that this strategic self actually keeps everything out: love, and all the good things in life, cannot enter through a defence.

Catherine:

One of my strategies is perfecting and performing, which started after my mistake in identifying the wrong brother as the one who sexually molested me. Performing well also worked to gain the attention and approval of my father. The problem is that even when the strategy works, it doesn't work. I know that if the whole world stood up and applauded me, there would still be a whisper from my basement that said, "If you really knew me, you wouldn't be applauding." If all my strategies worked with Duane and he fell to his knees and declared, "I love you, you are the one. I will spend the rest of my life gazing into your eyes, and I will never leave you," my basement would whisper, "If you really knew me, you wouldn't be saying that."

Duane:

My strategy, of course, was to be super in order to receive adulation and thus belonging. As a popular teen, I had a keen interest in a girl who I learned from others had an equal interest in me. After school we ended up lying on a couch together as I realized my dreams. My strategic self was indeed being loved and accepted at that moment. I couldn't stand it. I couldn't lie there. My entire body began to itch as if the couch were crawling with ants. I actually visited my doctor following this incident to consult about my skin condition. There were no ants and there was no skin condition. There was only a person who could not accept the very thing he wanted the most.

Have you ever achieved some goal you set for yourself and then wondered "Is this all there is?" Because we hold these SOSs, we end up resisting the very thing we want the most, even when it lands right on our doorstep. We do not allow the good things we have in our lives to enter because we don't feel worthy of them. When someone applauds our mask, it doesn't count emotionally because we aren't open emotionally. Our strategic self is not real: our real self is hiding in the basement.

In order to address what is in the basement, we must stop the harmful acting out/in behaviours we engage in. When we do that, what is hiding in our basement will make itself apparent.

Opening up requires opening the door to the basement, where this hurting aspect of our authentic self resides. We are frightened of being vulnerable because we are convinced that what we made up about ourselves is true. It is not!

What we hold in the basement is not all of who we are authentically, of course, but it is an important aspect of who we are. When we are brave enough to risk being seen, fully and deeply seen, then the good stuff can go to where we need it the most.

SELF-APPLICATION

Our strategic and acting out/in behaviours can kick in so quickly that we might not be aware of the anxiety that they are covering, which is revealed when we stop.

1. Take a moment as you go through your day to note in a journal when your strategic self is activated: when you get defensive or strategic, act out or in. At the end of the day, sit down and ask yourself what vulnerability the strategic self is guarding in the basement.

3 PROBLEMS AND RELATIONSHIP PATTERNS ARE MULTIGENERATIONAL (THE DISTANT PAST)

You cannot solve a problem from the same consciousness that created it. You must learn to see the world anew.
—**Albert Einstein**

YOU ARE BORN WITH A PAST

Who we are and what we believe is shaped not just by traumatic events from our early life; it is perhaps even more a result of the relationship web we are born into, our family system (extended family) or family of origin (the people we grew up with). For decades, psychology has debated between "nature" (genetics) and "nurture" (environment) in terms of what has more power to shape our personality and identity. Recent findings in epigenetics (the study of how genes are impacted by environment) make it clear that these two can't actually be separated: nature and nurture aren't different forces; they may well be the same force.

For example, did you know that you were present in your mother, in the form of eggs in her ovaries, while your mother was still in your grandmother's womb? Three generations occupying the same biological space. Family systems theory, synchronistically, tends to focus on how three generations of a family shape a person's identity and way of being in relationships. Research evidence has shown that traumatic or stressful situations experienced by a parent can change the genetic makeup of subsequent generations. The purpose of these epigenetic changes is adaptive: it is a kind of genetic preparation for entering a potentially hostile environment. Unfortunately, it can also be psychologically maladaptive, predisposing us to a particular fear-based pattern of thinking. *It Didn't Start with You* by Mark Wolynn offers a great reader-friendly summary of this research.

Whether or not you buy into the idea that the experiences of the generations before you have shaped you biologically, it is clear that our families have a powerful influence on our perception of the present. Rebecca Linder-Hintze, author of *Healing Your Family History*, tells a brilliant story to illustrate this point. One day she was preparing ham for dinner and her husband asked, "Why are you cutting the ends off the ham?" "It tastes better that way," she replied. She thought about this some more, then called her mother and asked, "Why do we cut the ends off the ham?" "It tastes better that way," her mother stated. The illogic of this response had started to become apparent, and eventually she called her grandmother to ask the same question. "I cut the ends off so it will fit into my pot," her grandmother replied.

We are taught how to perceive through the lenses of our family beliefs, from the time we are born. The qualities and characteristics of men, women, people, values, what is important in life and what isn't, what is allowed and what isn't: all of these are transmitted through our early relationships with family members. We do not perceive an objective truth, we perceive a subjective reality. We don't fully know this, however; even though this idea makes sense logically, there are so many of our own perceptions we automatically run with—thinking "that is just how it is"—that are simply not true.

> We do not perceive an objective truth, we perceive a subjective reality.

You are born into a particular family system, a particular web of relationships. Your family has a history and a way of being that predates your entry into it, and you are a cog that must fit into this system or relationship web. The moments that create these SOSs have a wide and historic relationship context around them. The other family players are also cogs in the same relationship web. All the players, past and present, have interacted in ways that shape your family's unique view of reality and way of being.

THE LEGACY OF LOSSES

Throughout the history of your family, people have experienced losses and hardship and have developed ways to cope with these losses. What the family values or holds as an important quality or characteristic is equally shaped by these losses. There have been many "something happened" or traumatic moments, and the construction of many strategic selves that came out of those moments.

It is rare that a family or individual within a family knows how or is given the space to fully process a loss; instead, survival becomes imperative. In the same way as an individual develops a strategic self, the family develops a strategy for survival on the foundation of loss, which (out of the best of intentions) is then transmitted to the next generation.

What we don't realize, however, is that in so doing we are also passing on the unprocessed loss: the fear and anxiety associated with the historic horrible event comes along with the strategy we are taught, even though we may not be aware of what actually happened back then. We are taught what to do to avoid ever experiencing that traumatic event again, and the "what to do" is transmitted from generation to generation more explicitly than the event that gave rise to it. The famous British saying "Keep calm and carry on" is an example of this kind of directive. It is saying "Do not feel or react; shut down and do what needs to be done." This guidance is appropriate for the Second World War bombings during which it originated, but is not appropriate otherwise.

We can also be "set up" by the family to make up for these old losses. In Duane's family, as we have seen, men were considered dangerous at worst and somewhat useless at best. He was highly praised, particularly by the women of the family, for being so unlike the men. He was set up to make up for the losses of the women by being Superman, the good one who saves rather than destroys. This wasn't conscious, it was simply how the system worked: it was looking for a "good man," and so he got praised for any evidence of being "so unlike his father." The more praise he received for being Superman, the more he became Superman.

We may also be set up to make up for a parent's losses out of the most loving intention: because a parent wishes us to have what they didn't have, and longed for. Catherine's mother had dreams of being a teacher but had to leave high school after her father's death to help support her mother and brother. Catherine has three university degrees. At one point following high school, she wanted to put off starting university and go travelling for a year, partially to have an adventure and partially because she actually wasn't sure what she wanted to study. This desire was not supported, as her parents feared she would not go to university if she did so.

The difficulty in this is that when you are set up to make up for someone else's loss in the family system, you will carry a weight of expectation, of dreams unfulfilled, that isn't actually yours to carry. You will be subtly or overtly directed away from things that might be more authentic for you and directed towards things others want for you or expect of you. Not only might this contribute to your own loss (because you sacrifice doing what you want), but you might not even know what you want because you have become more attuned to what is expected.

Catherine:

I like to think of myself as a control freak in recovery. One of my go-to control strategies is making plans. Before I make a move, I am wired to think about all the possible outcomes and how I would handle these. I have noticed a tremendous anxiety in myself that occurs when I don't have a contingency plan for a potential negative outcome.

Now, planning is not a bad thing. But in my case, planning is often driven by anxiety, and when there is an underlying anxiety driving a particular knee-jerk behaviour, or where there is anxiety if you don't enact a particular behaviour, you can be sure that there is also a historic loss at play. I don't have to go too far back into my family's history to understand that.

My grandmother on my father's side was left to care for her four young boys when my grandfather joined the army to fight in the Second World War. The story of how he joined is a curious one: he needed a hernia operation that they couldn't afford, and his understanding was that this operation would be provided free of charge should he join. He was told that he was unlikely to be sent overseas because of his age, that he would be able to serve within Canada. However, after recovering from the operation and going through training, he was sent overseas to be part of an engineering unit that ended up being put in some of the most dangerous positions there were. He suffered from shell shock (post-traumatic stress disorder) on his return.

There are many stories told about my grandmother during this time. She is a heroic figure in my family. She moved across the Prairies on her own in a covered wagon with her boys (who at one point lost the only money she had for food playing store in the back of the wagon). She was essentially on her own, having to find creative ways to survive—without a back-up plan. She did extremely well with this, but at the cost of a lot of anxiety and fear.

On my mother's side, a huge turning point for my grandmother occurred when she lost her mother to breast cancer as a child. Her whole life changed at that point. She emigrated from the UK to Canada at the age of fifteen and spent some time working before she met and married my grandfather, a farmer. My grandfather was apparently sick on and off from sciatica throughout my mother's childhood, and ended up in hospital in Winnipeg, a great distance from their small farming community. He died unexpectedly there at the age of 45 because of an allergy to the penicillin he was given. My grandmother was left in a difficult situation with her two children, and my mother, the oldest, quit school to help.

I believe I was taught to plan as part of the family strategy to deal with these unexpected events. That is why considering no plan leaves me feeling anxious about all the bad, unexpected things that could occur. I find myself visualizing all the bad things that could happen (that I need to plan for), and these bear a striking similarity to the bad things that I now know did happen in my family before my arrival into it. I end up feeling that old loss: I can easily feel far more anxiety than my real-life current situation warrants, because the high anxiety totally appropriate to the historical loss comes along with the planning strategy.

Duane:

My need to be super or exceptional, to make up for a deep sense of inadequacy, didn't start with me. It also didn't simply start from my experiences early on with my father's drinking. This drive to be exceptional, different, and noticed existed before I was born.

During the Second World War, my father had to remain on the farm while all his brothers went overseas to the front lines. This was the requirement at the time for families on a farm, as it would ensure that the farm would be tended to in the event that all the brothers were killed while at war. This might have been a welcome decision, given the prospect of possibly not returning, but not for my father. He always carried with him his fear that he couldn't prove his worth to his father.

One evening during my first year in university while studying psychology, I asked him about his relationship with Patrick Sr. He was in deep tears quickly, telling me of being left to tend the farm while the others were fighting overseas. I had no idea he was living with this. I was stunned.

His need to make up for this question about his worth was the same as mine. He was a showman and a risk-taker, albeit a very clumsy and, eventually, frightening one after a few drinks were consumed. Having an ambition to play professional baseball was a very outrageous dream at that time. When I look at the pervasiveness of alcoholism in my father's family, I often wonder what my father's father also wrestled with. He was also a risk-taker. He left all his brothers and sisters and his parents and emigrated from the comfortable textile industry in Northern Ireland to farming in the almost Arctic conditions of Northern Alberta. This was risky and adventurous.

My grandfather emigrated with his wife and first-born daughter, and by all accounts after arriving my grandmother quickly took control of all aspects of family and farm life. My grandfather's dream was taken over by my grandmother, and possibly this is where alcoholism first took root in my family system. In his bad drunken moments, this is the same accusation my father would throw at my mother: that she was responsible for the loss of his dream to be a professional baseball player.

I was also left with the sense that I had to defend my dreams from the women in my life. My focus on being a rock star was responsible for the demise of my first marriage. I am aware that I was attempting to make up for the shortcomings of my father, as I suspect he was also attempting to make up for the shortcomings of his father.

When a family teaches a strategy that is founded on loss, it also transmits the anxiety, fear, and unprocessed grief around the loss. The person receiving the directive might know nothing about what happened but still feel the anxiety.

FAMILY RULES, QUALITIES, CHARACTERISTICS, AND VALUES

The family develops rules to protect against these losses, which family members are overtly and covertly taught. Family rules may be the obvious spoken ones, such as "We agree to treat each other with respect," but more often family members live by the family rules and ways of being unconsciously. The family transmits its rules, reinforcing certain valued qualities and characteristics in its members and inhibiting others.

The strategies our family evolves exist to protect the family from painful experiences and losses. As a child moves through their natural course of development, they will inevitably encounter one of these hidden losses, and the family rule will kick in to govern the child. This might happen aggressively or it may be more subtle, but the message to the child will be the same: "It is not okay for you to be a certain way, you must instead do this. It is not okay to be angry: you must be nice. It is not okay to ask for too much/be greedy, you must be grateful for what you have." Here again, we take on suspicions about real selves, and our Behaviour C will be what is approved of or what works in our family of origin.

It is important to note that what works is not always the same as what is approved of. For example, an acting-out child who receives negative attention may be deflecting attention away from conflict between the parents. The black sheep of the family may provide an important focus point for other family members, who feel better in comparison. The reinforcement that occurs is not always obviously positive reinforcement.

There might be a family rule that states, "Do not take risks! Risks are dangerous." This may have come from a grandfather who recklessly lost the family fortune playing poker or a father who had an affair. There will be a rule and a subsequent message to a child that taking risks is wrong and dangerous: "Stay in line." Every time the child ventures into the world of expression or being alone, the parent may step in, believing they are protecting the child. But in that moment, the natural development of the child—their need to explore, to test and experiment—gets thwarted. The child fears rejection if they do not comply with the rules. The child becomes cautious.

It is important to emphasize that this is done out of positive intention: we wish to protect the current generation from experiencing the pain and loss of previous generations. Family rules and values govern every aspect of life, including how you think and feel about relationships, power, individuality, work and career, affection, feelings, control, freedom of expression, and so on.

Rules and values are necessary to provide a functional framework for all the members of a family to grow and learn how to relate to one another. However, the more unspoken, inflexible, and restrictive the rules of a system are, the more damage an individual living within the system sustains. Unspoken rules are transmitted covertly, through a process of disqualification or shaming. Disqualification happens when a person is "blanked out" in some way: their communication or behaviour is ignored, or responded to in a way that is invalidating. Inflexible means just that: the rule is not open to questioning or change and is seen in black and white terms. The rule doesn't change; people are expected to change to conform to it. Restrictive rules are those that do not allow for the full range of human experience. For example, certain emotional expression may not be allowed for some or all of a family's members ("boys don't cry"; "girls can't be angry"), or sexuality may not be acknowledged or discussed.

If the family is full of anxiety and fear based on historical unprocessed losses, the system will have unspoken, inflexible, and restrictive rules. There will be very little room for an individual to develop authentically. Instead, they will be at the receiving end of many moments when aspects of who they are authentically are shamed, invalidated, punished, or ignored because they have broken family rules. They will learn to adapt by incorporating the rules into their strategic self and playing by them in whatever way works for the family.

On the other end of this continuum, if the rules are spoken, flexible, and accepting, they will support the continued authentic evolution of all. Spoken rules may be discussed openly and are subject to comment and questioning. Flexible rules can change as times and people change and as values evolve through a considered process. There can be exceptions, rather than rules being black and white. They are accepting of all aspects of human experience. Real people grow out of such ideal family systems. Most of us end up with a mixed bag, aspects of self that are real and places where we hold SOSs and cover these with our strategic self.

The rules determine how a family deals with everything. Even if a trauma occurs outside the family environment, how the family deals with it will determine how it impacts you. We have heard many stories in our workshops of people being further traumatized by how a traumatic event was handled in the family. One woman talked about going home to disclose that she was raped at the age of 12 and having her father burst into a rage and load her into the car to drive the streets with a baseball bat beside him, looking for the perpetrator, all the while swearing, screaming, and saying he was going to kill this person. She was not taken to hospital until much later. Many children do not disclose sexual abuse to their parents, partially because they already know they are not to openly discuss sexual organs.

Conversely, even the most traumatic events may be processed through to completion in an open, supportive, accepting environment. It is not so much what happens that determines what we carry from the past, it is how difficulty is handled. Within the context of an open, accepting, connected family system, traumatic events do not necessarily have a traumatic impact.

> Within the context of an open, accepting, connected family system, traumatic events do not necessarily have a traumatic impact.

The rules are what govern the relationship contracts we have with those around us. The rules we learned in our family and hold on to determine how all our relationships unfold, and explain why we often end up experiencing the same thing with different people: we have the same contracts in the lines of our relationship network, even when the lines connect to different people.

Take a moment to reflect on your family rules and values. What feelings were allowed or not allowed? How were you allowed or not allowed to express these feelings? What could you talk about or not talk about? What was considered important and valuable in your family: career, education, money, power? Were there different rules for men and women? What is the ideal man, woman, or person according to your family perspective? How was affection expressed, or not?

The next time you get into a disagreement with someone, ask yourself how your family rules are playing into the issue. We are often confused and upset when someone else isn't following the rules we were taught and take for granted as simply being "reality."

DIFFERENTIATION: REAL AND STRATEGIC SELF

Based primarily on our family of origin's relationship dynamics, we end up living to a certain degree from our authentic, real self, and to a certain degree from our strategic, armoured self. The balance between these two is called "differentiation" in family systems theory. Our level of differentiation is measured particularly by how we are in the middle of anxious situations. High levels of differentiation equate to being able to continue extending more real self and less strategic self into our relationship web, and lower levels equate to extending less real self and more strategic self within the same level of situational anxiety. How long can you hang on to your authentic self? In other words, we all exist on a continuum between knowing who we are, making decisions from the inside out, and reacting to the environment or other people and adjusting ourselves depending on what is in front of us. The more you know who you are, the better you will feel!

The authentic, real self is non-negotiable in relationships, meaning that we don't change because of outside pressure, to meet someone else's expectations. Change occurs from an internal process, possibly considering feedback from others but not in any way due to wanting to conform or rebel: in other words, not because of a need to make any kind of relationship comment. All of us operate from our real selves to some degree. This is the self that was fostered and allowed to grow undamaged and uninhibited, where we hold no suspicions about ourselves. From this aspect of self we seek to give, and are honest, open, and transparent because there is no sense of lack or feeling of threat.

Our real self is also the one trapped in the basement, fearing that we are not good enough in our SOS (suspicion of self). The SOS is not real, but the person believing it is real. Here, we are frozen emotionally in time, having metaphorically locked ourselves in the basement: we may not have access and we definitely don't allow others access. It is very important to note that this part of ourselves has not gone anywhere!

We all operate to varying degrees from our strategic self, which has developed in lieu of the one trapped in the basement. The strategic self, made up of our mask and armour strategies, has as its purpose to hide (our SOS), to pretend, and to defend. To do that, we must be constantly reading and reacting to the environment and other people. We have discussed in detail the many ways we do so through our acting out/in behaviours. The strategic self seeks to get something from the outside world to make up for what we fear we are in the basement. The foundation of its existence is our SOS. We have our strategies, which are forever connected to what they are guarding in the basement.

> The strategic self seeks to get something from the outside world to make up for what we fear we are in the basement.

The more we operate from our strategy, the more anxious we will be. That is because the strategic self is reactive, constantly reading the environment to determine who to be and how to be. From the strategic self we are incongruent, meaning that who we are on the inside does not match how we present on the outside. If I do not know who I am, or I feel I need to protect, hide, and defend who I am, I will be anxious. The lower our differentiation level (or the less our real self emerges in the world), the more we will be engaged in trying to "do something" to make our discomfort go away. As we have seen, too often our actions end up amplifying the discomfort instead of alleviating it.

You will recall that we start to get used to a certain level of anxiety in the womb. The relationship dynamics in our early life set our anxiety thermostat to a level that feels familiar. Not good, but familiar. If a family interacts in ways that undermine the development of the real self, the family members will instead be constantly reacting to each other, and how they do that will keep the anxiety at a very specific level. Everyone cooperates in this game, although not consciously. Acting-out/in behaviours will kick in if things feel too bad or too good, in the same way that heat and air conditioning kick in to maintain a certain temperature.

It makes sense to people that we feel anxious when facing difficulty. But we feel just as anxious when facing success, celebration, and the good things in life. There has been much written about what happens to people who win the lottery, and statistically, winning the lottery tends to wreak havoc in winners' lives rather than improve them. They divorce, get depressed, go broke fairly quickly, and make poor, self-destructive decisions of all kinds. We believe this has more to do with differentiation levels than anything else. "How good can you stand it?" is an interesting question to ponder in this regard.

"How good can you stand it?" is an interesting question to ponder.

This is why we self-sabotage: we are looking to get things back to "normal," even if we aren't particularly comfortable with "normal." Part of the challenge in changing is learning to identify a new state as "home," or where we live inside ourselves.

The more real self we have developed, the less anxiety will drive decisions and behaviours. That doesn't mean we don't feel anxiety; in fact, the opposite may be true. However, when we are able to access our real selves, we gain the ability to feel that anxiety rather than kicking into behaviours designed to fix it. The more differentiated we are, the wider the range on the thermostat before the air conditioning or heat goes on. Learning to stretch your thermostat will prevent self-sabotage and allow you to accept the good things in life.

What we believe in our fear, we will keep spreading around through the relationship web. In fact, anxiety and fear are what fuel the particular patterns you gravitate towards in your own relationship system. We feel anxiety, and sometimes even before we are aware of it, our acting-out/in behaviours kick in, and the anxiety then begins to travel through our relationships, like passing a hot potato. It activates a particular circuit that everyone agrees to, regardless of whether they like it or not, and returns to sender.

INTIMACY: THE PURSUER-DISTANCER DANCE

The more strategic self we operate from, the more codependent our relationship contracts will be. We will require others to be a certain way so that we do not have to feel or face our SOS. What we refuse to work out for ourselves in our basements, we will require others to adjust to in some way to protect. The decision not to "go there" has major relationship consequences. There will be rules others must follow to be in connection, and those rules will undermine authenticity and growth.

> What we refuse to work out for ourselves in our basements, we will require others to adjust to in some way to protect.

It is important to note that "real self" or "highly differentiated" does not mean "independent" in the way we glorify independence in popular culture. Highly differentiated people are interdependent: they have a realistic sense of their essential connection to others and are able to both hold on to self and be close. The less we operate from our real selves, the more we look to have a self reflected back through another's eyes, or we need to preserve a safe emotional distance to have a self.

Another way to think about all this is in terms of intimacy. How close can you allow someone to come? The more you have locked in your basement, the further you will need to keep others from it. Regardless of what you think you want, the degree of intimacy you end up experiencing in all your relationships is the one you enforce.

Each of the acting-out/in behaviours we have discussed is a particular dance step in an overall game designed to sustain a familiar, learned, "safe" distance from people who are important. People who are important have power, and that, we believe, is dangerous. We want to be important to others, but we do not want them to be more important to us. We engage in a tricky negotiation that says, "I will make you only as important as you are willing to make me. You are not allowed to make me less important, and I certainly don't want to make you more important."

All of this happens because of how the past interferes with our perception of the present. We are unconsciously doing this juggling act because of all our memories about what happened when someone was important and had power. Our experiences in the basement wake up as soon as someone becomes significant to us. This, of course, acts out profoundly in romantic relationships, but anywhere that power dynamic occurs is equally vulnerable: with our boss, with our children, with our best friend.

How we maintain the "right" distance is also tricky. The degree of intimacy you end up experiencing, regardless of what you think you want or what you think you are capable of, is the one you participate in creating. The simplest way to explain how this all works is to use the pursuer-distancer metaphor. Underlying every relationship dynamic is the pursuer-distancer dance. The pursuer is the one who wants to be closer, and the distancer is the one who avoids.

The pursuer often thinks they are much more capable, willing, and able to be intimate than the distancer. But, weirdly, pursuers connect with distancers. If in fact pursuers were more capable of intimacy, they would attach to another pursuer like Velcro and be incredibly, blissfully close. That doesn't happen, because the real purpose of the dance isn't intimacy, it is distance. The "pursuit" is part of a dance designed to sustain a distance.

When we fall in love, for example, we feel like we are instantly close. "We talked all night!" couples will frequently exclaim when asked to describe the beginning of their relationship. But this isn't real intimacy. In the early stages, this is more an engagement with the fantasy—what might be or could be—rather than with the reality of the other person. As two people slowly come closer over time, at some point they will hit the wall where they can go no further (because they never learned how to get any closer in their family of origin).

Here is a fact that will twist the minds of the pursuers in romantic relationships: we only fall in love with those who understand the exact distance we learned to maintain in our family of origin. Despite pursuers believing themselves to be capable of more intimacy (remember, wanting intimacy is different than being able to achieve it) and often believing they know what needs to happen to achieve it (the other person has to change), they are exactly the same as the partner they complain about—no more or less able to be genuinely connected. The dance wouldn't be happening if one person was legitimately more capable of intimacy and connection.

Both positions in the pursuer-distancer dynamic are driven by the strategic self. Both are ways of defending self that are not based on authenticity. The pursuer is looking to have a "me" through a "we," by having a self reflected back through another person. The distancer is looking to protect a "me" by avoiding the "we," believing that they will lose self if they let someone get close. These aren't necessarily fixed positions: people can trade roles. Often when the pursuer gets tired and gives up, the distancer becomes the pursuer.

> The pursuer is looking to have a "me" through a "we," by having a self reflected back through another person. The distancer is looking to protect a "me" by avoiding the "we," believing that they will lose self if they let someone get close.

We actually have two related fears about allowing someone close to our basements. One is the obvious: we don't want anyone to see who we fear we are because if they do, we fear we will be abandoned, rejected, punished, or found lacking in some way (just like when…). We also fear allowing someone power, allowing someone to be important. In our attempts to avoid letting someone have power, we withhold our love. We refuse to give because we don't want what we give to make us vulnerable.

This is a really important thing to realize: we are not only trying to hide, we also actively hold back from contributing positive feelings and giving ourselves fully to our relationships. We are just as frightened of the good as we are of the bad. If it gets too good, we fear losing it, and we would rather just have it be mediocre or even bad, believing that if we don't let it be too good we won't feel the pain of loss. The fear of loss comes from our personal experience around what happened when someone was important, and from the legacy of loss in our family.

THERE ARE NO GOOD GUYS OR BAD GUYS: REDEFINING THE PROBLEM

Hopefully it is becoming apparent that when you get into trouble in relationships, both people are contributing to the dilemma. Always. There are no good guys or bad guys in these dynamics. We get into "good guys and bad guys," who is to blame and who is not, because we don't understand the cyclic, patterned nature of our interactions. We split our interactions up into cause and effect, and see the other's behaviour as the cause and our response as the effect.

Catherine would say that she had to pursue, remind, cheerlead, and eventually criticize Duane because of his avoidance and distance. She had to overfunction because he never stepped up to the plate. Duane, however, would say that because Catherine was all over him all the time, he had to avoid and distance. It was the only way for him to have a self. Neither of us was causing the other's response; instead we were caught in a negatively reinforcing relationship pattern, or feedback loop.

Underlying this feedback loop are all kinds of beliefs that we feed into the system. When we are stuck in a feedback loop like this, it is because all the solutions we try are based on the same underlying assumptions and so create the same result. For example, Catherine's cheerleading and criticism are very different behaviours, but they are both founded on the same underlying fear in the basement ("I am not enough, I must do more, I must have your acceptance and approval to be okay"), and both transmit the same relationship message. The same is true of Duane: his avoidance, distance, and threats are very different strategies, but all are founded on the closely held belief that love is a threat that will eventually hurt him.

This perspective on the problems we face is revolutionary, if you stop to think about it for a moment. Problems never exist in isolation: there is always a reinforcing relationship component. There are no good guys or bad guys, no heroes or villains, because there is no first cause. This doesn't mean that destructive actions are okay, of course, but if we can see the action in the context of the relationship landscape surrounding it, we can change the pattern. We are no longer victims of the effect of the villain's choice: we have power to evolve the whole system by taking responsibility for who we are in the middle of the dynamic.

In order for anything to legitimately change, we have to begin by redefining the problem. There is a lovely saying in the 12-step Alcoholics Anonymous program that goes, "My very best thoughts got me into this mess, why would I turn to them now?" Or, to paraphrase Einstein from the beginning of this chapter, we can't solve a problem from the same mindset that created the problem. Changing the definition of the problem allows for a new solution. The problem is what you hold in your basement, which you end up transmitting into your relationship web, which then sets up a negatively reinforcing situation with the people around you.

OUR STORY

Although we both have expertise in the helping profession through education and years of experience, our ability to be truly helpful to others comes more from the fact that we have learned something along the way, facing and moving through our own struggles. This book is not intended to focus on romantic relationship, but a significant aspect of our story is about how this played out in our personal relationship(s).

Catherine:

When my basement was being formed, I found solace in books. I started with fairy tales as a young girl, then graduated to Harlequin romances when I was a teen. I lived through the characters and longed for my own happy ending. The promise I read between the lines of these stories was this: I am lacking and not good enough, but when I find "the one" who will love me, then I will finally feel good enough.

I brought all my well-learned strategies to my formative romantic relationships, and very little of my real self. I performed, overfunctioned, and adapted myself to what I thought the other wanted. The first boy I fell in love with as a teenager was a typical "bad boy," who told me directly that he would not fall in love with me. That suited me just fine, because if I could get this hard-to-get one to love me, then maybe I would feel worthy. Of course, that was destined to fail spectacularly. He was chronically unfaithful, and I adjusted for years, feeling more and more unlovable as I sacrificed myself in pursuit of his love.

I did my best to live the life that I felt I should, applying my perfectionistic skills to my education. I met the man who would be my first husband at university, while I was still with my first boyfriend. I suspect I might not have left my first boyfriend if I hadn't had my future husband to move towards. He presented as the opposite of my boyfriend: he was considerate, and in fact was the son of a Presbyterian minister, so would fit into my family well.

A key experience that brought us together was a personal-growth workshop with a spiritual framework, which we did in the company of several of our friends. For me, this was life-changing on many levels. I felt that I had found my calling (I determined that I wanted to facilitate similar workshops), and for the first time felt some freedom to be the real me. I decided I wanted to be called Catherine at this workshop, rather than Cathy, the name I grew up with.

Sadly, I didn't learn how to be my real self in the real world, and quite quickly returned to my strategic self. I had no idea at the time what the problem was, but from my current perspective it is clear that I had no clue what it meant to be my real self behaviourally, and so I fell back into what was familiar. My life and relationships continued to organize themselves around my strategies. For example, my future husband confessed some time after this workshop that his main reason for attending was that he thought I was "cute," and that he really didn't buy into the spiritual framework presented. I adjusted and started to sacrifice what was important to me in the same way I had with my first boyfriend. I felt alone, and was unaware that my own strategies were feeding that experience because I wasn't letting anyone near the real me.

I continued to lead the life I thought was expected of me. I graduated with top marks from my clinical psychology graduate program, I married, I became pregnant with my daughter. I felt more and more flat and lifeless and had no idea that it was because "I" wasn't present in my life, my strategic self was. The more depressed and anxious I became, the more I exerted my control strategies and tried to move my life in the direction I thought it needed to go for me to be happy. The more I exerted my controlling strategies, the worse I felt.

The universe eventually intervened with a rather dramatic exercise in letting go of control, in the form of a mystical near-death experience I had while giving birth to my daughter (more on that in Chapter Eight). Following this traumatic and enlightening experience, I was both elated and lost. I now had a visceral sense of a loving force greater than myself, but the life I had constructed with my strategies was at odds with what I now knew. Unfortunately, this also created a gulf in my marriage, because my husband was clear that he didn't share my spiritual beliefs. I was wrestling to integrate what was for me an earth-shaking experience and couldn't talk to him.

As a result of this experience, the first year and a bit of my daughter's life was the opposite of the preceding flat years. I was up and down like a yo-yo. I was totally in love with my baby girl, could recall my mind-blowing experience in detail, and also fell into pits of despair trying to figure out who I really was and how to rebuild my life on this new inner foundation. I didn't have words to describe my experience and didn't feel I had anyone to talk to. This is the context in which I first met Duane.

Duane:

Throughout high school I was known as "the untouchable." I was a musician and an athlete, and popular; I found safety in being sought after but never found. It wasn't as though I avoided relationships consciously. Believing I just had high standards, I thought I never met the right one. I didn't have high standards; I was scared. I suspect my model for intimacy had more to do with reading Archie comic books than anything in the real world. I wanted to live on Elm St. in Riverdale and date Veronica or Betty. Riverdale was a dream of the simple, pure, and uncomplicated. It posed itself as an answer to the Elm St. I came from, which was more of the nightmare variety.

I would seek, find, and run at the first sign of serious attraction coming back my way. I met my first wife shortly after I graduated from high school. She had just moved into the neighbourhood from New York, which could have just as easily been Riverdale to me.

Chapter Three

Her combination of not instantly coming my way, being American, and being very cute completely captured me. The more she ran, the more I longed for her and wrote some great songs. This chase lasted for a few years, bordering on the obsessive.

It also launched my musical career. I left the country when I was 22, travelling to London as a musician in an attempt to become distracted from the pain of being denied. It didn't work. I just wrote more songs. After I returned to Canada, the relationship she was in was becoming abusive and she turned to me for support, which I provided, being Superman and a professional counsellor by this time. Shortly after that, she finally fell in love with me and declared as much to me. The moment she uttered the words "I love you," I fell out of love. The irony of this didn't escape me, but nonetheless I started distancing. I couldn't stand it. My skin started to itch.

After a number of months of pursuing me, she gave up and intimated she was done and was considering starting up with someone else. I fell apart and proposed. After four years of marriage and continuing to chase me, and tired of watching me chase my musical career instead of her, she called it a day for good. Again, I was crushed.

I had absolutely no idea what was driving my bus, but clearly the depth of my struggle in the basement was running my life, making certain that no one could get close to me on one hand, and on the other, projecting the solution outside, pursuing women that didn't want me.

A few years later, I met another wounded bird that also looked like the girl next door in Riverdale. My career as a therapist and a musician remained in full swing as she presented herself, on the way out of a failing relationship and enamored by my Superman-like qualities. She had a difficult past with her schizophrenic father, who had sexually abused her and her two sisters. Abandoned by her mother prior to entering grade school, after years of sexual abuse she finally left home at 14 to take care of herself and her younger sister. My story couldn't hold a candle to the insanity she had lived through. She was looking for someone to be the answer as much as I needed another wounded bird to be the answer for.

For two weeks it was an extraordinary match made in heaven. It soon became hell. Neither one of us could stand being this close for too long before the drama set in. It didn't take long for my Superman qualities to seem more like Darth Vader to her. As I moved closer to the history and the depth of the pain in her basement, she started to blame her inability to be close on my disappointing actions and shortcomings. I was stunned. This was the first time I wasn't running the other way. Her finding fault in me woke me up to the pain of my own SOS. My ultimate fear was that being a disappointment put me in the same category as my father. A failure. My Achilles' heel. This became an identity crisis at the level of my strategic self. If I was not Superman, then I had to be Darth Vader. There was nothing in the middle. I couldn't leave until I had changed her mind about me. I thought this was love. I wrote some more songs.

The following 13 years can be best described as being on a roller coaster without any brakes. The pursuer-distancer dance continued, with both of us spending an equal amount of time in both positions. The relationship ended on 20 different occasions over that 13-year stretch. Whoever had been left would be ready to enter a treatment centre, and the one who had left would be planning a trip to lie on a beach in Waikiki. We did both. I preferred the vacation spot over a padded cell, but in the last few years of the relationship, the cell became my permanent residence.

She upped the ante with numerous affairs. I became clinically depressed. I had no other cards to play. By this time, my father had committed suicide a few years earlier, my younger sister Laverne had been killed in a car accident, my musical career was over, and any financial security I had possessed had been lost in the Vancouver *stock market crash. I had traded my cape in for a cup, metaphorically begging my family and friends to hang on to me, as I feared falling deeper into the abyss.*

As pieces of my identity as a hero and musician were falling off the shelf with the durability of fine china, I feared that every incremental loss of the shattered remains on the floor was evidence that I was losing myself. I didn't realize until much later that I actually wasn't losing myself. I was losing my strategic self. In the end, the only thing left was my real self.

I left the relationship and didn't look back, despite her desperate calls to rescue her from the cell with endless promises of renewed devotion. This time I had taken an enormous step, finally having a long-overdue face-to-face with myself in the basement. The quest now was also a spiritual one, I having witnessed a near-death experience with my soul. For the first time, I believe I had reconciled my worth and my sense of identity straight-on, rather than entering yet another pursuit of yet another unattainable woman, writing yet another song, or, equally, entering another 100-metre dash in the opposite direction as yet another woman started seeking me out. I accepted the fact that I might never be in a relationship again, and that was okay. I had myself, finally.

I started lecturing about my recovery. I spoke passionately in front of hundreds, intensely describing the profound possibilities of healing and learning from my near-death experience on that roller coaster. I was profoundly grateful to be alive again. My private practice soared as I wrote therapeutic processes rather than songs. I started Clearmind. I travelled the world. I was on stage and popular. I was figuratively on a train finally going somewhere rather than a roller coaster going nowhere. I looked up. There was Catherine.

Catherine:

Duane was giving a lecture a friend had brought me to, about relationship and spirituality. I was so excited about the approach he was describing because it made sense of what I was struggling to integrate and offered some insight into how to live. I felt like I had found my home in the work he described, and the calling I had glimpsed years before.

At first it was a huge relief to have someone to talk to, but very quickly I began falling in love. I was honest with my husband about what was happening and didn't lie or cheat, but the process of sorting through my feelings, my husband's feelings, Duane's feelings, and what it all meant was a painful one for all involved. Eventually my husband made the call that we should separate, and I agreed. Once again, I had moved from one relationship to another.

Our daughter was two and a half at that time, and our extended families were understandably upset. For the first time, I was either a) admitting I had made a huge mistake or b) about to make a huge mistake. Either way there were major repercussions, particularly for my daughter. This certainly activated my basement fear that I was horrible and dangerous (from when I identified the wrong brother as my abuser).

Duane and I came together, and I had something to prove: that I had not made a horrible mistake (and therefore that I was not a horrible, unlovable person). Because of my need to make this relationship work, I once again fell into many of my strategies, even though I knew better. We eventually moved in together and then hit a wall. The issue in our relationship was how much time we spent together.

Recall that my dad travelled a lot when I was younger. Strangely (or not), I ended up with a man who was very much the same: passionate about his work and travelling all over to do it. I would pursue by suggesting time we could spend together, suggesting things we could or should do, and in response Duane would avoid and distance.

When my cheerleading attempts failed, I would eventually get critical, in my subtle, passive-aggressive way. My style was to be a prosecuting attorney. Rather than make a statement, I would ask a leading question; for example, if he was late for dinner, my comment would be "Do you know what time it is?" (I am a very difficult person to argue with!) My clever criticism hit Duane right in the basement: my clear communication was "Look at how unhappy I am: you are failing."

Duane would aggressively argue back, which would eventually escalate to the statement that was guaranteed to get me to back off: "You know, Catherine, maybe this relationship isn't working." That one hit me right in the basement, where I feared I was unimportant, unlovable, and a problem—or, perhaps even more horribly, I had made a mistake! My instant strategic reaction was to back off, adapt, and make everything okay again.

Duane:

When I met Catherine, I was lecturing on the deeper purpose of healing wounds in relationships. I spoke with vigour about the treachery of the mistakes we make and the price we pay when we look to fill ourselves up with the rapture of another. After this talk, Catherine told me how impressed she was with the material and subject matter. If anyone could find her way through all that I had been through, it would be someone like Catherine. She possessed an elixir of intellectual pedigree, softness, loyalty, stability, and a quiet yet firm commitment to never revert to drama and hysteria as a means of dealing with conflict. Are you kidding me? She was also physically beautiful, which sealed the deal. I was in.

Once again, I stood on a stage priming my strategic self. This was my most coveted meeting place for gaining approval and acceptance. Whether it was serving Mass on the altar of a Catholic church, a strutting pyrotechnic musician promising adventure and passion, or behind a podium offering the best in cutting-edge psychology, the intention was the same: to present a strategic self in lieu of my authentic one.

My message was that I now knew how to be in a relationship, but in truth I wasn't nearly as able as I had hoped. I certainly knew of the difficult waters and the relief of having not drowned in them. I still did not know how to swim. It didn't take long to find that out. My guard was up and ready for the first sign that I was failing. All hands on deck. It didn't take long. My history of being criticized and coming up short was long and dramatic.

Catherine presented her feelings in a much more appropriate manner: her most outrageous moment and worst day may still have been better than my ex's very best day. She was, and is, that good. I recall we were having a relatively civil argument early on in our relationship—by the car, as I was again running somewhere. On my end, I am sure I was pushing things too far about the space I required. Catherine was holding a cup of coffee and responsibly tossed it in my general direction. It was a precise toss, ensuring that it would land on grass rather than concrete and not within the proximity of any living creatures, including me, ensuring safety for all. The grass would also take the coffee as water. That was it.

I couldn't count on her histrionics to point at to explain my need for distance. That was difficult. Nonetheless, once more I was witnessing in a woman sadness that, deep down, I could have confessed—but rarely did—was all my fault. This quiet drama carried on for quite some time, with Catherine predictably adapting, morphing, sacrificing, and doing all she could to make it work, to avoid her own anxiety, while I was matching by leading these dance steps with an equal and opposite amount of running, hiding, avoiding, and subtly explaining the problem as her being too needy. She should get some help.

"Maybe this isn't working out," I would occasionally but strategically say. I would say this not to end the relationship, but more to bring it back to a comfortable distance, where Catherine would retreat back into being polite and assume responsibility for managing these difficult passages for both of us.

Catherine:

We got stuck in a particular dance step that kept us at a familiar emotional distance from each other. Despite the fact that our family stories were very different, both our families defined the emotional distance associated with intimacy in the same way. Neither of us had learned how to be any closer than what we achieved, and both of us, despite all our training, were inclined to attribute the problem to what the other was up to.

SELF-APPLICATION

See if you can catch a relationship pattern in action. We are blind to relationship dynamics because we focus on the content of a difficulty instead of watching the relationship process. Ask yourself what is happening underneath the content. These were the dance steps in our example above: Catherine overfunctions, cheerleads, plans, suggests; Duane avoids and distances; Catherine gets passive-aggressive and subtly critical; Duane attacks and threatens; Catherine moves the goal posts, backs off, makes everything okay. Catherine overfunctions, cheerleads, plans, suggests; Duane avoids and distances... Both end up reinforcing their own and each other's SOS in the basement.

Part Two: REAL

The world breaks everyone and afterward many are strong in the broken places.
—Ernest Hemingway

It is easier to love humanity as a whole than to love one's neighbor.
—Eric Hoffer

4 PROBLEMS MUST BE RESOLVED IN RELATIONSHIPS

We are disturbed not by what happens to us, but by our thoughts about what happens to us.
—**Epictetus**

Catherine:

When Duane and I were in that stuck pattern in our relationship many years ago, we had both been practicing therapists for years. We were good at what we did. We had already formed Clearmind, were already engaged in teaching workshops, and our work was spreading to different locations all around the world. This is all to say, we knew better!

I was aware that I was collecting evidence to "prove" that I was not important. I was aware that Duane's focus on travelling and work was "just like when" my dad would be gone or work-focused when I was a child. In our calm, less anxious moments, we talked about this. We understood what was happening. Unfortunately, as we have seen, these patterns are not driven by our intellect, they are driven by anxiety. Neither of us was prepared to face our anxiety. When push came to shove, we both acted out and in.

Until I had a showdown with myself. One day, after Duane had made one of his not-so-subtle threats implying that this relationship wasn't working out, I took a good look at myself in the mirror. What was I doing? I moved the goalposts, adjusted, and backed off, all in an attempt to preserve the relationship. I overfunctioned in an attempt to prove my value. But all I was really doing was proving my lack of value, because every time I did more than my 50%, I was telling myself, "Who I am is not enough." I was non-verbally asking him over and over, "Am I good enough yet?"

I thought if I made myself necessary, needed, I would be chosen, or wanted. I had made myself necessary very quickly with Duane: I had inserted myself into every aspect of Clearmind, from writing workshops and facilitation to administration. I had placed myself in every part of his life.

With a sinking feeling in my stomach, I realized that being needed and being wanted were different things. I let myself for the first time consider the possibility that maybe this relationship wasn't working. If Duane wasn't happy, if he was telling me the truth, then what was I doing trying so desperately to make it work, essentially all by myself? Maybe I ought to respect what he was saying instead of constantly trying to change his mind. Maybe if he wasn't happy with me, I ought to let him find his happiness instead of trying to control him.

As soon as I considered that possibility, I was flooded with fear. What was I really afraid of? As humbling as it was to admit it, I realized that I felt like I needed this relationship to work, and I needed Duane to love me, so that I could believe I was loveable and okay. I was looking to have a "me" reflected back through the "we." I was also terrified of potentially having made a mistake, just like when I made a horrible mistake by identifying the wrong perpetrator as a child. I was engaged in trying to make it work so I wouldn't have to face being mistaken. This was the anxiety driving my behaviour, and I admitted to myself that this was harmful both to me and to Duane.

From there, I knew what I had to do. I hung on to myself really hard, sat Duane down, held his hand, and said, "I love you. I want this relationship to work. And the next time you say to me that you don't think this relationship is working, I will believe you."

EEEKK!

PROBLEMS ARE OPPORTUNITIES TO GET UNSTUCK

The places where we get stuck are not just a problem, they are also an opportunity. We are stuck in those places for good reason. Every single problem we face in life is also a point of evolution if we stop long enough to let it make itself known to us. The emotional discomfort and pain that we refuse to face can teach us, if we let it.

Understandably enough, people wish to avoid pain and pursue pleasure. However, our emotional system doesn't work that way. Unfortunately, if we want to be able to feel better, we have to get better at feeling all feelings. Period. The emotions we distinguish as "bad" use the same network as the ones we equate with "good." Anger/passion, fear/excitement, sadness/empathy—if you think about it for a moment, aren't these emotional states quite similar? Someone who is sobbing is only a hair away from someone who is laughing. To move to what we all want on the positive end of the spectrum requires allowing the so-called negative feelings, as they are the starting point.

When you have a headache and take a pill to treat the headache, you don't actually address the root of the problem. Just as physiological pain can be a signal that something is wrong, so emotional pain can be a signal that something is off and needs correction. Too often, we don't pay attention to the initial mild discomfort. Instead, we continue doing all the same things to alleviate our anxiety, expecting a different result.

The acting out/in cycle escalates, and eventually the pain becomes so overwhelming that we have to pay attention. Alcoholics hit rock bottom, marriages dissolve, overfunctioners suffer a "nervous breakdown" and have to take a leave of absence from work. Too often we wait until the situation is desperate before we are willing to pay attention to what the pain is telling us.

The pain has a purpose. The pain is there to provide direction to the basement, where some very important aspects of self have been locked up because we are holding on to mistaken beliefs. The whole system of defence that we have erected—the mask, the armour—only makes sense if what we fear in our basement is actually true. We never go there long enough to question, is it, in fact, true?

> The whole system of defence that we have erected—the mask, the armour—only makes sense if what we fear in our basement is actually true. We never go there long enough to question, is it, in fact, true?

As Epictetus said, "We are disturbed not by what happens to us, but by our thoughts about what happens to us." Human beings heal reasonably well from events, but the meaning we make of these events is what we carry forward from the past into the present. We are in charge of that, period. Others did what they did, but what we are choosing to believe as a result is entirely our own creation. This meaning, which is not just cognitive but also emotional, is at the root of our suffering.

These beliefs are the foundation for our behaviour. Our behaviour reinforces our fear-based beliefs. Changing our minds and behaviour can start an upward spiral. However, as we said in Chapter Two, these beliefs are more accurately feelings as opposed to thoughts, as they were formed at a time when we were wired to operate primarily from our emotions. So we must visit the basement emotionally and change what we believe, using the feelings as a portal to identifying the beliefs.

Memory is encoded through emotions. What we learn in a particular physiological-emotional state, we will remember best when we are in the same physiological-emotional state. Psychology refers to this as "state-dependent learning and memory." This is partly why people who experience traumatic events like car or plane crashes will often have gaps in their memory of the event. This is also partly why those who experience trauma in childhood may not remember the event. (We say partly because the process is more complex, but this is one aspect of it.)

When we stop our acting-out and -in behaviours and allow ourselves to feel, we can use those feelings as a thread to discover "just like when" we felt this way earlier in our life. This is what Catherine did when she faced herself first and acknowledged that the current situation was triggering her fear of making a mistake and being unlovable—just like when she identified the wrong perpetrator as a child, and just like when her dad was unavailable or lost his temper when she wanted his attention. These feelings, and the beliefs that are hidden within them, have been around since long before the person you may be currently blaming for them.

Emotionally, and sometimes quite literally, we end up

returning to the scene of the crime, meaning that we end up replicating the feelings and sometimes events we are trying to get away from. This is because we have to be where we are before we can get to where we want to go. We stopped our natural evolutionary or developmental process at that point, and we must return to the same place to continue our evolutionary or developmental process.

> We have to be where we are before we can get to where we want to go.

We have to turn away from our strategies on the sidelines, turn our focus away from him, her, this or that, and turn to face the real source of the problem in the basement.

LET YOURSELF BE VULNERABLE WHERE YOU ARE VULNERABLE

Carl Rogers said, "The curious paradox is that when I accept myself as I am, then I can change." Rather than hide our fears (SOSs) by locking them away in the basement and donning a strategic personality, we have to turn back to the basement and let ourselves be vulnerable where we are vulnerable. The basement is only a basement because we are hiding our fears. Hiding and/or defending produces more of the shame and guilt we are trying to alleviate. Without masks or defences, our fears become simple human vulnerability.

> The basement is only a basement because we are hiding our fears.

In Chapter One you identified your SOS and the "just like when" attached to it, the story that put you in the basement.

You have also identified the strategies and defences you evolved to hide your SOS. Understanding this is helpful because this understanding invites a certain degree of self-acceptance. We do the things we do for good reason. Why wouldn't you be this way, considering where you came from and what you have been through?

Insight into self is only the beginning; the next step is to actually allow yourself to move through those historic feelings. The dilemmas we face in life are helpful, because they allow us to tap into the emotional underbelly of the whole system. In our experience, when we actually let ourselves feel, rather than constantly interfering with the process, our emotions move fairly quickly. We cause ourselves suffering not because of the historic pain but because of our resistance to it—all the strategies we employ to avoid it or numb it the minute we feel it.

All our SOSs were made up in a moment of disconnection with another human being. They occurred in relationships, often with someone who was important to us. They surface in relationships with other human beings as well. Rather than hide, pretend, and defend, we have to learn to embrace our own vulnerability and allow ourselves to feel what is triggered. We have to be willing to drop our defences and strategies and allow the person in the basement out.

This requires practice. Sometimes it will require professional help. Learning to allow vulnerability is a scary proposition because we are so convinced that we will be punished or attacked in some way. But as we have seen, it is our defence that creates the experience of punishment.

Duane:

When Catherine responded with "the next time you say that, I am going to believe you," she broke all the rules of this relationship, and I stood shocked. I am sure she was as well. I would never have said that to her while believing that I actually meant what I was saying. I had no intention of actually ending the relationship; it was more that it brought things back to a comfortable closeness and distance that I could live with. She would typically fall back into moving the goal posts for me, so that I didn't have to feel the discomfort of the closeness and she didn't have to feel the discomfort of potentially being alone. I waited two days for her to return to playing by the old rules and moving the goal posts again, but it never happened. I was posed with the dilemma of upping the ante—of accusing her of giving me an ultimatum—or telling her the truth. I chose the latter. I had come to a place in my life where this had become an all-too-familiar pattern. I wasn't leaving this time. I asked if we could talk.

"Catherine, every time you ask me if I know what time I am going to be home, I have to visit the home I came from first. When you seem unhappy I feel like a failure, just like my dad. That is where my upset really is. I didn't know that. I have been punishing you now for what happened to me back then. That isn't fair. I have no right to do that. You had nothing to do with it. I am sorry. All you want to do is create a home for us. I am so scared of what you will find in me, that I am a failure, like my dad...defective. I run, hide, and blame you for any of the problems, including accusing you of being needy. That is wrong and irresponsible. I have a problem. This is my problem. I am finally taking responsibility for what is my pain. I love you. You will never hear me suggest to you ever again that you are the explanation for my pain."

Catherine:

It was so apparent to me when Duane showed his vulnerability that the opposite of what he feared was true. The person I saw in that moment was brave, beautiful, and perfect. I can't remember if I said anything about what I was seeing, but I am certain I communicated all of this clearly on a relationship level, through my eyes and the tears streaming from them. There was nothing but love inside of me at that moment for him.

After Duane's demonstration of vulnerability, I followed suit. "I am also sorry. I realize I have been trying to manipulate and control you. I am so busy doing everything because underneath all that I am horribly afraid that I am unlovable, and so I think I have to earn love all the time. I am constantly trying to prove my worth because I am afraid that I don't have any. I am scared that you are going to find someone better out there and that I will be alone. I'm scared that no one wants me, really, and my only way into relationships is to make myself valuable to the other person. I'm scared that if I'm alone, it really does mean that I am not good enough.

"I'm sorry that I have been trying to get you to cut your travel. The man I fell in love with was travelling all the time. When you head out on a trip, I see my dad walking out the door again. That isn't your problem, that is my problem. I commit to taking responsibility for that instead of trying to get you to rescue me from my pain by being different."

The irony is that when we actually show ourselves vulnerably, it is glaringly apparent that our SOSs are lies. The person who is revealed emerging from the basement is as pristine as when they first decided to lock themselves up in there. Another person's eyes become like a mirror, reflecting back this truth. At a relationship level, the communication is clear.

CONNECTION IS REQUIRED FOR CORRECTION

That was a powerfully connective moment for both of us and a major turning point in our relationship. That moment transformed not only our relationship but, even more significantly, how we felt about ourselves. What we know to be true about who we are now matches what we feel to be true (although we continue, like all humans, to be works in progress).

Vulnerability is connective. Brené Brown has written extensively and beautifully on this, and we have seen the truth of that over and over again in our personal and professional lives. When someone is legitimately vulnerable, our hearts open. We care. That caring extends itself to the person in front of us, and a connection is formed. We say "legitimately vulnerable" because vulnerability does not carry a "victim" energy, and it is not need.

Because our suspicions of self were made up in relationships, they must be corrected there as well (meaning in connection with another human being). We can read all the self-help books we like and understand the intricacies of how we operate, but without connection, that will leave us in a constant argument between what we know to be true and what we feel. We will be split, knowing better in our head but feeling something different emotionally. We will constantly be trying to talk ourselves out of our feelings.

The feeling of connection is the correction for these suspicions of self. Not so much the affirmation, the "you are good enough," loveable, or whatever, although these words spoken by another human being (or oneself) are a helpful anchor. Recall that 80% of communication occurs at a relationship level, and only 20% is content. It is that powerful, non-verbal

80% that carries the day here. The aspect of self we sentenced to the basement has been disconnected, suffering in isolation. The feeling of connection pulls us out of the basement and back into life.

The feeling of connection pulls us out of the basement and back into life.

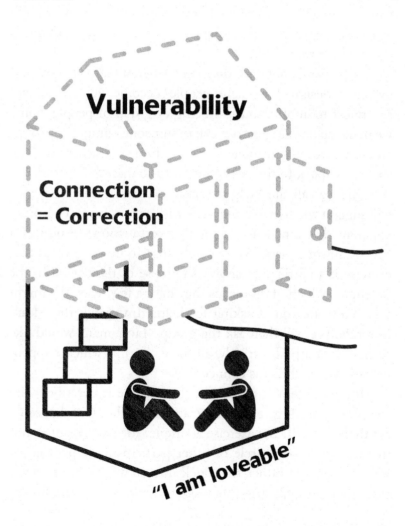

Over the years, we have come to realize that our therapeutic skill is best directed at helping people become vulnerable, because most people don't know how to get there on their own. Sometimes we don't even know we have a basement, we are so used to the flat existence we experience from our strategic self. Once a person is vulnerable, what happens between human beings is natural. We have often said we don't do "healing work" so much as "revealing work," because once vulnerability is revealed, healing occurs. We pick up again at the evolutionary point where we left off.

In our workshops we do many experiential processes and exercises designed to help people become vulnerable and reconnect to another human being or group of people. Some we make up on the spot to speak to someone's unique dilemma, and some we have formulated and continue to use because they so clearly speak to themes common to so many.

One we call the "help me" exercise. This is an exercise we will suggest when in our interview with a participant it becomes apparent that a person commonly overfunctions to protect a fear of unworthiness. We will only start to move towards that exercise if a participant shows a glimpse of the person in the basement, which often means they have a few tears. We might ask, "How are you at asking for help?" Invariably, they don't, as a rule. We will then ask the group, "How many would like to help [name]?" Invariably, all hands go up (which happens because vulnerability is connective).

The purpose and process of the exercise is described, and the participant is given a choice about whether it makes sense for them to try it. The exercise is simple. The participant stands in the middle of a circle of other participants, supported by a facilitator, and rather than kick into strategies to avoid the fears that naturally arise, they ask for help with them. So, for example, often the first thing is "Will you help me to learn that it is okay to ask for help?" All the participants who affirmed their desire to help respond, "Yes, I will help you," and the person in the middle then has to decide, looking into the eyes of those around them, if they will accept the help. If they do, everyone takes a step forward.

Are you cringing as we describe this? That is because closing the gap of physical distance will activate the person's fears around emotional intimacy. Again, rather than sidestepping to avoid the fear, we support them to allow their vulnerability to surface, and ask for help with it. We often move to requests like "I feel unworthy of your attention, so will you help me to remember that I am worthy?"

We typically continue the exercise until the person has reached the core of their vulnerability and gotten emotionally in touch with their SOS. The real person in the basement has emerged. People have moved closer. There is a powerful feeling of connection and care in the room. The participant in the middle is asked what they see in the eyes of those surrounding them—is it what they fear? "No, people are caring…" Who are they looking at with such care? What do you imagine those eyes are seeing as they look at you? "Someone who is worthy…"

Essentially, we are helping them to notice and feel the connection, which then leads to correction. Connection and correction happen simultaneously. We learn to accept ourselves when we see others' genuine acceptance, and we learn to love ourselves when we receive others' genuine caring. We must do the work of choosing to believe and allow the new experience, which then dictates a new way of being. The words spoken during these kinds of processes are helpful to be able to integrate the experience, but the felt experience is what makes the difference.

This is what is required for healing. We have to risk allowing ourselves to be seen, deeply and vulnerably seen. We have to be willing to challenge our fears, rather than letting those fears drive our decision-making in life. When we do that, the love and care others extend has somewhere to enter. We can accept and receive the good things in life we are surrounded by. Love cannot enter through a defence, or a strategy, but as soon as we are willing to open the door to the basement, it floods in.

Whenever we give talks on this subject, someone will inevitably comment, "That's all very well, but vulnerability doesn't work in the real world!" Actually, in our experience, it does work in the real world. But it takes skill to learn to communicate responsibly in this way (coming up in Chapter Five), and there are no guarantees. Sometimes the one on the receiving end of your emotionally responsible vulnerable communication will react from their own triggers and history. The guarantee we can give you is that vulnerability will always work better than defence.

THROUGH FEAR TO LOVE

It is scary to be vulnerable. That fear is literally the portal back to connection and love, as will hopefully be illustrated for you as you begin to practise. There is no way around; we must go through. What we must go through makes itself apparent in the moment we move towards connection again, towards allowing ourselves to step into unknown or unfamiliar intimate territory.

> It is scary to be vulnerable. That fear is literally the portal back to connection and love, as will hopefully be illustrated for you as you begin to practise.

As in the help-me exercise we described, we have to start from where we are and gradually peel back the layers of our fear, allowing the process of moving towards our fear to reveal ourselves to us. In essence, we have to be willing to let go of control and allow. It is more a feeling of allowing the process to unfold, as opposed to directing it.

We must be willing to follow the path back to our authentic self, the path that we pioneered away from. We experienced a trauma of some kind, we took on a suspicion of self, and we developed a defence system, a strategic personality, designed to keep ourselves and others away from what we are hiding in the basement—all founded on the notion that what is hidden there is bad, wrong, or flawed in some way.

As we moved away from our SOS in the basement, we developed more and more finely honed strategies and defences. Those defensive actions, as we have seen, are not neutral. Part of the healing required is to take accountability for what we have been up to in our misguided actions. Alcoholics Anonymous acknowledges the importance of making amends in the healing process, which is Step 9 of the program. It is vital to change our mind about who we are in the basement, to correct those suspicions of self, and it is equally vital to take responsibility for any harm we have done to others.

As we discussed in Chapter Two, all attack and blame is projected guilt and shame. And the more we attack and blame, the more we feel guilty for our actions and shameful: this amplifies our suspicion of self rather than alleviating it. The more shame we feel, the more we turn to our insane strategies, and the whole cycle escalates.

Brené Brown, among others, has said that guilt is healthy if we feel it for a moment and then act on it by apologizing or making amends. It is perhaps semantics, but we would prefer the word "remorse" to describe that feeling, which is a noticing of and instant regret for the impact your behaviour has had on another. It is the feeling attached to "sorry."

Guilt can so easily become self-obsessive and self-attacking instead of other-focused. We have in our work seen many people, attempting to be accountable for their behaviour, who get caught in this self-attacking state rather than truly being focused on the other, and weirdly, often the one wronged is then put in the position of having to take care of the other's guilt.

There is a big difference between accountability and guilt. Accountability springs from remorse, which comes from having a clear view of self ("I made a mistake") and other ("... which impacted you"). Good people make mistakes all the time. Mistakes are correctable, but being a horrible person is not. Correcting these mistakes by apologizing will go a long way towards helping you feel like a better person. Correcting our mistaken suspicions about ourselves is only part of the equation when it comes to healing and evolving ourselves. When we change our beliefs, we change our perceptions. We notice in our world that which is consistent with what we believe. What we do also changes, because the behaviours that naturally arise from this new way of thinking and feeling will be different behaviours.

Real change requires addressing what you think, what you feel, and what you do. Any one of these three interrelated aspects of our being has a potential evolutionary point. If you change what you do (behaviour)—for example, by stopping your acting out/in or by repositioning in relationships—you will become aware of feelings that you have been hiding from and thoughts that you have been keeping secret from yourself. Change what you believe about yourself in your basement and your old behaviours no longer make sense. New behaviours will more naturally follow. Change how you relate to your own uncomfortable feelings by inviting them rather than trying to inhibit them, and you will become aware of the fearful thoughts attached to those feelings.

> If you change what you do (behaviour)—for example, by stopping your acting out/in or repositioning in relationships—you will become aware of feelings that you have been hiding from and thoughts that you have been keeping secret from yourself.

DEFENSIVE STRATEGIES CAN BECOME TOOLS

Behaviour is often habitual, and if you do the hard work of correcting your underlying SOSs in the basement but fall back into old ways of being, you can also erase the hard work you have done. It is really important to make conscious decisions about your behaviour, reviewing what makes sense for you in light of how you are deciding to live.

All your defensive strategies can be used for a different purpose when you change your mind about who you are and where you are going. Nothing about us is essentially wrong or bad. When love, trust, and friendliness is driving the bus, our learned strategies can become positive tools in our toolkit.

For example, one aspect of overfunctioning can be a kind of hypervigilance. In order to overfunction in relationships, you have to be very aware of what others are thinking and feeling (sometimes more aware than they are), to anticipate what it is that you think you need to do. This awareness, or radar, when driven by fear is destructive to self and other, as we have seen; but when driven by genuine love and care, this awareness becomes empathy and the basis of therapeutic skill (helping someone do for themselves).

We are aware that we have asked you to take some significant steps in applying what you have learned in this chapter. Take some time with it, and journal about the results. It takes courage to act on what we are suggesting here, so be gentle, move at a reasonable pace, and allow yourself to integrate the experience.

SELF-APPLICATION: VULNERABILITY EXPERIMENT

We are going to ask you to take a calculated risk with this one. Review your basement story (the newspaper article and headline from Chapter one), and at the end of it, write a sentence saying "I made this event mean that I am... [SOS—the headline to the story]." We are going to ask you to read your basement story to a friend, one who has earned your trust and whom you feel safe with. Before you do so, let them know that your intention is to take a risk by sharing a painful moment from your childhood with them, and that you aren't expecting them to fix you or make you feel better. You simply want to be able to share it. You will have only one question at the end of it, which is "Does this change how you feel about me?" Tell them this up front, and ask if it is okay for you to proceed.

If the thought of this exercise fills you with such terror that you can't even imagine doing it, then you can do a rewrite and pick a story that feels risky but not overwhelmingly so. You could also bring your story to a qualified professional therapist (ideally one trained more in relational/experiential therapies). Or both.

Read your story to your friend and ask the question "Does this change how you feel about me?" Try to look up as you read, and at the end when you ask, you must look at your friend as they answer. Repeat back what you heard them say: "I am going to repeat what I heard you say so I know I understand. I heard you say.... Is that right?" Tap into the 80% relationship message; what do you see in your friend's eyes? Don't forget to thank your friend for participating in this experiment with you!

If your friend has also read this book, even better—you can do this exercise together. We often have a fear that sharing at this level will push people away, but the opposite occurs: people feel closer.

This exercise is a calculated risk, because you are deliberately moving into a closer connection with someone who has shown themselves to be safe and trustworthy, so it has a 95% chance of success in terms of your experiencing the connection and correction we describe. However, regardless of the outcome, you can be proud of having taken this risk! Doing this exercise requires that you challenge your own fear first and foremost, and you can be proud of the courage you displayed in taking this risk.

5 Evolution Through Connection: The 5 Skills of Emotional Responsibility

Never doubt that a small group of thoughtful, committed citizens can change the world; indeed, it's the only thing that ever has.

—Margaret Mead

Vulnerability is the birthplace of connection and the path to the feeling of worthiness. If it doesn't feel vulnerable, the sharing is probably not constructive.

—Brené Brown

Emotional responsibility

The number-one feature associated with being an adult is responsibility. Our hope is that when you realize that you are always connected, and that every move you make has an impact on those around you, the gravity of this responsibility becomes apparent. What you don't work out in your basement, you will require others around you to caretake in some way. You will have rules in your relationships about what you can and can't talk about, what is and isn't acceptable. You may even require that everyone keep out entirely, believing that the only safe place to be is alone.

The "small world" phenomenon, more popularly known as "six degrees of separation," states that any two random people in the world are connected through a surprisingly few acquaintance steps (three to six, on average). We have been discussing your relationship web as if it were a contained entity of known people, but in fact we are all part of a network that extends between all beings. You have influence over people you haven't met. Our ability to impact each other through this network isn't bounded by location or by direct contact.

Think about how this applies to our global human network for a moment. You may be physically located at a distance from the war zones of the world (or you may not be), but you are not so far away on a relationship level. The way the world operates right now is a result of what we are all putting into this web. Many of us have terrorists inside our own heads, if we are honest, and regardless of the (very important) fact that we do not act out in that way, the message still communicates. Consider what you think and how you behave when someone cuts you off in traffic.

We so commonly wander around assuming we have no, or very limited, power, but that is simply not true. At a relationship level, everyone has equal power and influence, no matter what the outward appearance or the designated structure. The lowliest administrative assistant has as much influence as the CEO, at a relationship level, when they say hello on the elevator. Some of our greatest leaders, such as Martin Luther King, Nelson Mandela, Gandhi, Mother Theresa, Pope Francis, and Malala

Yousafzai, to name a few, have come from apparently less powerful social strata.

> At a relationship level, everyone has equal power and influence, no matter what the outward appearance or the designated structure.

We have no choice about whether we have power and influence. We have choice about how we will wield our power and influence. Do you want to be helpful or harmful?

We have to start by taking 100% responsibility for the state of our own existence. No matter how others have impacted and influenced you—and they have—after you reach adulthood, the choice as to who you are and what you will do in response is entirely your own. You are the only one who gets to determine what you will put into the relationship web, and what you put in or give determines how you feel, no matter what the actual outcome. If you are emotionally responsible, you will feel good about yourself when you walk away from even a difficult interaction, because you will have put something positive into the system.

Emotional responsibility requires practice and skill, because we all exist in little systemic pockets that operate with varying degrees of irresponsibility within a greater global system that operates primarily through fear. The world looks the way the world looks because of what we are all up to. We don't know what we don't know! We don't know how to operate from vulnerability rather than defence. This chapter introduces you to the five skills of emotional responsibility; if you put these into practice you will change your life, guaranteed.

Non-linear systems theory (chaos theory) has a concept popularly known as "the butterfly effect," which makes the point that very small variations, such as a butterfly flapping its wings on one continent, can affect the weather pattern on another continent. Small changes can produce big variations or changes. *A Course in Miracles* states that "there is no order of difficulty in miracles." Miraculous occurrences can begin from small variations on the positive end of the equation.

SKILL #1: CONTAINMENT

Containment refers to your ability to feel—and particularly to feel uncomfortable emotions—before you act. When something happens that triggers us, too often we react, because that trigger seems to just "pull" that reactive behaviour from us. We have to learn to create a space between the triggering event and our reaction to it. We have to learn to stretch our anxiety thermostat so that we can handle emotional discomfort.

In our work, we often advise people to "sit in your anxiety," meaning feel it rather than try to fix it. It is scary to feel those uncomfortable feelings because we are so convinced that something bad is happening. We are convinced because way back then something bad did happen, and so now we react to our own fear instead of proactively addressing whatever is happening.

Remember when your parent advised you to take a deep breath or count to ten before you responded when you were angry? This is good advice! We need to learn to do all we can to create some space between a triggering event and our response to it.

The practice of containment, of not reacting, requires emotional awareness as its foundation. Just the act of labelling a feeling can decrease the emotional intensity of it. As with everything else, we learn to label our feelings in childhood. A parent might notice a certain expression on our face and ask, "Are you feeling sad?" In this way we learn to put a label on a particular felt experience. This requires a certain amount of attunement on the part of our caregivers.

Despite Western culture aspiring towards gender equity, how boys and girls are raised continues to be different, particularly when it comes to feelings. Not only are boys not allowed vulnerable feelings to the same degree, they often don't get the same training to label their feelings. Physiologically, men experience emotion with the same degree of intensity, but they may not appear to feel because they lack the ability to put words to these feelings. Because women continue to be socialized more towards relationships, they are trained to be more sensitively attuned to feelings and to label them.

There are any number of simple emotional-awareness meditations on the Internet which assist in becoming aware of the felt sensation of a given emotion. The more practice you have in simply allowing your felt experience, the less these emotions will drive you in your daily life. You will recognize them when they occur instead of having them activate an internal alarm that then activates a patterned behaviour. The act of labelling a feeling decreases the intensity of it, allowing you to do something proactive rather than reactive, which leads us to our next skill.

SKILL #2: REFLECT VS. RELOAD

As we move through life, we constantly encounter situations that fire off a predictable reaction: we are "triggered." We all have our unique triggers, because we all have our unique life experiences, and only those who resemble the difficult aspects of our past in some way will be a trigger.

> As we move through life, we constantly encounter situations
> that fire off a predictable reaction: we are "triggered." We all
> have our unique triggers, because we all have our unique life
> experiences, and only those who resemble the difficult aspects of
> our past in some way will be a trigger.

When a trigger activates a particular feeling and you are
able to contain your experience within, it is an opportunity
to reflect (instead of reloading your familiar strategies). As
we explained in the last chapter, the feelings that surface in
a moment when you are triggered are a window to the past.
In those moments, someone is knocking on the door to the
basement, and you can use your upset over a current situation
to discover what beliefs want to act themselves out.

When we are triggered, we are using the current situation
to prove our fears. This doesn't mean that difficult and upsetting
things don't happen; of course they do. But if the current
situation is a spark, our past is like gasoline that we throw on
top of that spark. Human beings are capable of handling even
the most difficult losses and events if we resist the temptation
to draw negative, destructive conclusions about them.

1. When we contain our feelings and reflect, we have a
   chance to ask ourselves some very important questions:
2. What do I fear is happening?
3. Therefore, what do I fear this situation means about
   me? Is my fear true? (No!)
4. What can I take responsibility for?
5. Conversely, what will I not take responsibility for?

These are the questions we both reflected on in that
turning point in our relationship many years ago. Catherine
feared that Duane did not want her and was leaving, and that
she was therefore unlovable and not good enough. She took
responsibility for her own pain and for the control tactics

she used to prevent Duane from leaving. She stopped taking responsibility for making the relationship work, beyond just doing her part. Duane, ironically, also feared that Catherine was leaving. (Many people do actually leave relationships in an attempt to pre-empt the other person!) He feared this meant that he was a failure. He took responsibility for his distancing tactics and his own pain.

The point of reflecting is to turn your focus inside rather than continuing to focus on what is happening outside of self as an explanation for your pain.

Skill #3: Vulnerable communication

Vulnerable communication is the art of telling the truth in an emotionally responsible way, meaning without blame. Rather than hide, pretend, defend, or offend, the goal is to communicate honestly what is happening inside. What a shocking concept! Hopefully it is apparent by now that the overriding message in any communication is the relationship message (versus content), and we cannot lie at that level anyway.

Vulnerable communication will always feel risky, because it is real. It is vulnerable to say "I love you" first. It is vulnerable to say "I'm sorry." It is vulnerable to say "Can we talk?" In these kinds of communications, you are revealing yourself and the importance of the other to you rather than trying to "protect" yourself.

Vulnerability is attractive, because when we are legitimately vulnerable, we are being real. What we are believing in our vulnerability may be mistaken (our SOSs), but it is attractive because, even so, others are seeing your real, unhidden self. We will never be attracted to masks in the same way, although we can be temporarily taken in by them.

The degree to which you bare your soul to any one human being is a judgment call, but we all need at least a few relationships in which we can let our most tender parts be seen. It isn't healthy to "overshare" in a relationship that has not earned your trust, but at the same time trust is a process that evolves out of risking vulnerability. Relationships develop into vessels of transformation when one person takes a vulnerable step, is met by the other, who also takes a step, and so on until a bond of trust is formed.

Healthy, emotionally responsible, vulnerable communication exists along a spectrum that starts with stating a relationship intention, moves to taking accountability, and ends with transparency. The first two of these can be done in any relationship, whether it be at work, with friends, or at home.

> Healthy, emotionally responsible, vulnerable communication exists along a spectrum that starts with stating a relationship intention, moves to taking accountability, and ends with transparency.

The first prerequisite for vulnerable communication is a positive relationship intention. As we have seen, if you are speaking just to be right about a person or situation, it isn't vulnerable, it is defensive. So every vulnerable communication should start with a declaration of what you want in your relationship with this person. for example, "I really want us to have a good working relationship" or "You are really important to me as a friend/partner." Can you feel your own vulnerability as you consider even these kinds of communications?

The next step in a vulnerable communication is accountability. Here you are focusing on your own contribution to the relationship dynamic you are wanting to speak of, and owning that. Accountability should have the feel of an admission, for example, "I have been thinking about what happened the other day, and I realized that I was making you wrong. I'm sorry. I want to try and listen to what you have to say." It is not only appropriate but necessary to be accountable as a starting point for any conflict resolution.

The prerequisite for vulnerability in any potentially difficult conversation is that you have to be willing to be wrong. This doesn't mean that you are wrong, but you must be willing to be wrong. If you can maintain a position of being willing to be wrong, you will stay open to what is actually happening in the present. It is a way of alerting yourself to pay attention. If you aren't willing to be wrong, you are in defence. You won't be open to any new information, won't be seeing the person in front of you accurately, and will be invested in justifying your position.

At the end of the vulnerability spectrum, where we feel the most risk and invite the greatest benefit, is transparency. Where accountability has the feel of an admission, vulnerable transparency has the feel of a confession. Transparency means that you are revealing yourself at your most tender place and inviting the other to see and know you there. This will involve telling the other about who you are and the history of what you are feeling and believing about yourself at the trigger point. The degree to which it is appropriate to be transparent depends on a number of factors, such as how much trust is present and whether the role you are in with that other person allows you to lean on them emotionally.

It is not appropriate for a parent to be fully transparent with a preteen child, for example, as that creates a reversal of roles requiring a child to take care of the parent. As a child matures, it is appropriate to allow the relationship to transition into one where a parent's humanness is evident. It may not be appropriate for a boss to be transparent with an employee. It is always appropriate to be transparent with close friends and committed romantic partners. If transparency is not welcome or safe in those relationships, then there is something wrong.

In our experience, however, transparency is appropriate in far more circumstances than people are typically willing to consider. If we are ever going to change our culture to one where everyone's vulnerability is welcome and safe, we are each going to have to do our part to step outside our comfort zones. While it might not always be appropriate to fully allow your felt sense of vulnerability into every relationship, it is always appropriate to share the wisdom of your struggle, meaning you can talk about your own vulnerability and what you are learning there. You can talk about the basement without actually opening the door to the basement.

Taking 100% responsibility for your own state translates into using "I" statements when you are communicating your experience. When you use "I" statements to convey your experience, it decreases the chances of making your pain someone else's responsibility, which also makes it easier for the other person to hear your message. We can get tricky about that, as we shall see.

Using "I" statements to describe your experience is also a clean way to stop crazy-making arguments. Others can argue the facts of a situation, but no one can argue your experience. It would be crazy to say "No, you don't feel that way!"

Incidentally, "I feel that you..." is not an "I" statement! It is imperative that we differentiate victim communication from vulnerable communication. Victim messages are not attractive and do not invite, because they contain an underlying relationship message of blame: "You did this to me!" Vulnerable messages convey something more like "This is where I am living inside my basement. It isn't your fault; you are just knocking on the door." Using words like "hurt" or "disappointed" are tricky in this regard, as it is so easy for another person to hear "you did this to me."

Let's take a look at some examples. Consider for each if you would be drawn towards the other person or if you instinctively want to step back.

"I am really disappointed that you are cancelling our date night. I was really looking forward to it. I feel like we don't get to spend enough time with each other." How would you feel if you were on the receiving end of this? Can you discern the subtle element of blame here? How about this instead: "I really value our time together because you are important to me. I am sad that you're cancelling our date night. I will miss you." What kind of a response might this communication draw from you? The first statement is subtly guilt-inducing, and the second, because it is emotionally responsible, is more likely to receive an accountable response. You could choose to add more transparency to this statement and invite the other to get to know you at a deeper level by adding something like "These kinds of situations can really activate my fear of not being loveable, which started way before you ever entered my life" (as a starting point for a more in-depth conversation).

"I was really hurt that you didn't acknowledge my hard work on that presentation." How would you feel on the receiving end of this? How about "You know, I really value our working relationship and your feedback. Boy, sometimes I take lack of acknowledgement really personally. That's my stuff, has a whole history for me way back. I noticed that you didn't say anything about my presentation; can we talk about that? Is there anything I need to know or improve?" The second draws you in, doesn't it, and could be the start of a very important conversation. Perhaps the other would respond with an "I'm sorry, I was distracted and I meant to say something!" or perhaps there is information they could then provide to help you improve. You would want to know that, right?

We presented this example at a workshop on vulnerable leadership recently, and one of the participants asked, "Why do you even need to say the first part, about your history? Can't you just say the second part?" For two reasons: because it is true, and will be communicated covertly if you don't acknowledge it overtly; and, more importantly, because the degree to which you are willing to be vulnerable equals the strength of the connection you invite.

"I am feeling really overwhelmed. Sometimes I think if anything is going to get done, I have to do it myself." Overfunctioners might make this statement, particularly the second part, covertly instead of overtly. From an emotionally responsible perspective, a vulnerable statement would be "I really want to learn that I am part of a team, and I know you're an important member of that team. Sometimes I can be a real control freak, and I work myself into overload because I fear that my value lies entirely in what I produce. I want to learn how to let go and share the load more reasonably, because I know you are capable." If you don't know that the other is capable (because you are so busy overfunctioning), you could say "because I never let you show your capability." Or leave that part out.

These communication steps of stating the relationship intention then moving to accountability and possibly transparency may seem mechanical at first; however, they will gradually work their way into your communication style with practice. You will find the results well worth any potential initial awkwardness.

SKILL #4: DOING 100% OF YOUR 50% IN EVERY RELATIONSHIP

We are often asked "When do I leave a [romantic] relationship?" Our response is always "After you have shown up in it." This applies in our mind to all adult relationships, whether friendships, family, or work. "Showing up" means bringing your self to the relationship, fully and responsibly, rather than focusing on what the other needs to change. The irony about overfunctioning is that the overfunctioner isn't showing up any more than the underfunctioner. The overfunctioner is busy occupying the other but isn't occupying themselves.

"Mind your own business" is really good advice. Doing 100% of your 50% means showing up fully, yourself, doing the tasks that are yours to do, and backing away from minding another person's business. It means identifying what you will take responsibility for and what you will not take responsibility for. It means being, yourself, what you want the relationship to be, considering self and other equally. When you are able to do that, it issues an invitation to a healthy dynamic.

For overfunctioners, this means leaving the gap. The reason we overfunction is because of our own anxiety that the other will not step up to the plate. And others will not instantly step up the moment you back away. Overfunctioners must turn and face their own anxiety here, addressing their own fears and SOSs rather than shifting the focus onto the other. We must address our fear of not being good enough, which won't even surface as long as we are focused on the other not being good enough.

When Catherine delivered her "the next time you say that, I will believe you" statement, she was backing up to the 50% line, determined not to keep meddling in Duane's business to convince him that she, and the relationship, was okay. That was only the starting point, because Duane's two days of introspection that followed were excruciating. That is the gap that would normally be instantly filled by Catherine moving the goalposts. The minute you fill the gap, you're done: you're back to the old destructive dance.

Here are some examples of overfunctioning statements transformed into vulnerable communication. "You know, you've really got a problem. You should go take a workshop with Clearmind!" This one is a pretty obvious attempt at controlling the other. The vulnerable communication could be something like "When we get into these conflicts, I get really scared about our relationship. I realize I have a problem: I don't know how to connect. I start telling you what to do because I don't know what to do. I feel really alone."

"Oh, don't worry, I know you're busy. I'll take care of making all the arrangements for our trip." In a personal relationship, the vulnerable communication could be "I realize I was about to offer to take care of everything. Sometimes I get scared that I am not good enough as I am and fear that I have to do things to prove that I'm worth loving." In a professional relationship, the accountable communication could be "I know you're busy and so am I. How can we handle this so that we are both okay?" Or, to add vulnerability to the mix, "You know, I really struggle to believe that what I have to give is enough without overdoing it. Too often I feel like I have to prove my worth. That is a pattern for me. I'd really like to do something different here."

For underfunctioners, this means giving words to the gap instead of using the avoidant or distant tactic that is often so automatic. In a workplace situation, this might sound something like "I have a fear of failure that can really push me around, and so I can easily hide behind others taking the lead.

I can sometimes then hold them responsible for whatever goes wrong. I am committed to learning how to fully step up." In a personal situation, it could be "I often fear that I'm just guilty and wrong, so I get scared to say or do anything because I fear it will just be a mistake and make everything worse."

Now, those who gravitate to the underfunctioning role can choose to step up at any time. However, for those caught in this (two-person) dance, it is often the overfunctioner who finally manages to shift things. They do so by leaving the other person's problem with them instead of taking responsibility for it. They leave the gap. The gap we are referring to here is the amount of time that would normally elapse before the overfunctioner kicks in, as per the relationship's established pattern. The underfunctioner won't start to feel their own anxiety until that time passes; in the meantime, the overfunctioner's skin is crawling. For both, the task is to hold on to self and to take responsibility for self.

We are often asked about boundaries, particularly when we start talking about vulnerability and doing 100% of your 50%. Where do you draw a line around another person's behaviour? From our perspective, a boundary will be naturally occurring when you operate from your real, non-negotiable self. It is not a line you have to draw so much as the person within that you have to find. Equally, you have to be able to see the other as worthy.

A healthy framework is one in which we are considering self and other equally. Catherine drew a boundary, and this arose from her determination to believe that she was worthy, as well as from respect for Duane's worthiness and right to find happiness in whatever way made sense to him. Doing 100% of your 50% means letting go of needing to control the outcome. Do 100% of your 50% and let the world sort itself out around that.

> A healthy framework is one in which we are considering self and other equally.

SKILL #5: ASKING FOR HELP

At our healthiest, human beings are interdependent creatures. We are already connected, and we function at our best when we are operating in connection in an emotionally responsible way. We are all on a path towards evolution, and we maximize the benefit of this for all when we practice these five skills.

When we get into trouble, this means asking for help. This might mean asking for honest feedback from a friend on how you handled a situation, and then going back based on what you learn and doing some clean-up (because if you don't go back to where the mess was created, this is triangling). This might mean taking a workshop or getting professional help. None of us knows what we don't know. Change requires new information.

There is a big difference between asking for help and asking for rescue. Most of us ask for rescue: "Rescue me from my pain by not doing things that will trigger me. Instead, do things that will fill up the sense of lack I have inside me. Tell me how wonderful I am. Promise you will never leave. Be the good ending to my bad story." The rules we establish in our relationships are rescue devices designed to help us avoid our pain and anxiety. Our comfort zones are the same.

> There is a big difference between asking for help and asking for rescue. Most of us ask for rescue.

Asking for help is "Help me with my pain by reminding

me that my fears are not true. Help me to challenge them and get bigger than them instead of staying in my comfort zone. Remind me that I am already enough as I am, and I will do the hard work of learning to believe that." When we are vulnerable and asking for help, people want to give.

The help-me exercise we described in Chapter Four is a good example of the process. Perhaps the most vital step in this is the question "Do you accept?" How you answer that determines whether you are asking for help or rescue. Help is just that: assistance. If a hand is extended to you, nothing will happen if you don't take that hand. Psychologically, this means opening the door to the basement and allowing the help to come in by making what we are discovering in the present our new reality.

Imagine being the person in the middle of that exercise. You have just looked at the caring group of people around you and asked, "Will you help me remember that I am good enough as I am, that I don't need to be perfect for you to accept me?" The response you get is "Yes, I will help you remember that you are perfect just as you are, flaws and all." More important than the words, you can see that the people around you are loving you even though you have let them see what you feared were the worst parts of you. Can you let it in? Can you believe that maybe you are good enough no matter what mistakes you have made in this life, even though you may be an imperfect partner, an imperfect parent, and so on?

This is the transformation point: how much will we let it in? In some ways it doesn't matter whether, on a scale of 1–10, we are letting it in at a 2 or a 10. What matters is that we are building a new foundation and taking responsibility for that foundation ourselves. When you refuse to let anything in, you are asking for rescue. But if you are struggling to let it in, at a

2, you are taking ownership of the struggle and starting, even if it is hard.

Here is a potentially new thought: the people giving the help benefit as much as those receiving. There isn't actually a separate giving door and receiving door: they are one and the same door. We all have a need not just to be loved but also to give love. It is in giving that we learn that what we have to offer is valuable. When someone accepts our help, we feel good, because in the moment that they are acknowledging their own worth, they are also acknowledging ours. Sometimes we feel that this is the hidden secret of our successful workshops: not so much that people get what they have been longing for, but rather that people learn to give what they have been longing for. They get to experience their own power by witnessing the impact that what they give has on others.

That is also why it is hard to be in relationship with an overfunctioner in any context, whether it be at work or at home. We all have a need to feel as though we are contributing to our partner or the other, and when we are met with the message "I don't need your help, I can do it all myself," it erodes our sense of value and worth. Asking for help allows others to contribute.

COURAGEOUS CONVERSATIONS

Things happen in the present that need to be talked about. Employees are consistently late for work or don't meet expectations. Spouses betray each other. Mistakes happen. Everything you think and feel isn't just a trigger from the past: there are real events that happen that also require feelings to be expressed and worked through.

Too often our attempts to talk about something tangible that requires resolution become destructive because of how our past plays into the dynamic. If the triggering issue is a spark, what we bring from our past is like gasoline on that spark. We end up charging a person for manslaughter when they were only jaywalking or parking in the wrong zone.

Being able to disentangle the past from the present allows current dilemmas to be addressed proactively, in a way that facilitates everybody's growth and evolution. Our "if you say that one more time" conversation is a good example of this. The conversation Catherine initiated after reflection was necessary for the evolution of both of us, and was addressing a real issue. It took courage for Catherine to express her love for Duane and draw a healthy boundary. It took courage for Duane to reflect and then apologize and commit to a new behaviour.

It isn't enough to change our minds, we must also change our behaviour. As we have seen, our beliefs have a life in our relationship network: our relationships organize themselves around what we put into them. Courageous, emotionally responsible conversations are one of the ways in which a relationship system can evolve into a new, healthier dynamic. We cannot keep our new belief without anchoring it in a new behaviour.

The following example is an issue that we had with one of our international staff. This was real, intense, and of the high-stakes calibre.

A few years ago, we contracted with our Liverpool sponsor to become our UK sponsor, with the hope of extending our workshop locations beyond just Liverpool and into other cities as well. Jacquie had shown remarkable networking ability in the Liverpool area, and we hoped that she could extend the same approach and ability towards the country as a whole. However, in order to accomplish this, she would need to leave her full time position as a supervisor in a recovery facility and take on more of a full time position with our company.

A fairly wealthy member of our community decided to support the plan by being willing to finance her wages for a period of a year, on the premise that books would be kept up to date, progress would be made, and that by the end of the year three other UK locations would be established, with workshops held more frequently. This was a substantially large risk and commitment on the part of this person, who was motivated by his love of Clearmind, but also a large risk and commitment for Jacquie, embarking on a lifestyle she longed for.

As the months went by, we noticed that despite having more opportunities for communication, workshops, and lectures, we were in fact having less communication, contact, and results. We were becoming very anxious, first and foremost concerning our relationship with our benefactor and our friendship with him, and secondly for the dream of extending Clearmind further into the UK falling flat on its face. Thousands of English pounds were appearing to be going nowhere.

After approximately eight months, Jacquie ended our arrangement prior to the agreed twelve months, citing logistical difficulties. As we discovered later, Jacquie had also been having relationship difficulties with people involved with Clearmind, who appeared to resent that she was now employed by the company. We did not have this information at the time, and could not understand her justification for leaving. It was tense.

In the middle of this, Duane was scheduled to travel to teach a workshop at which Jacquie was assisting, in London.

Duane:

I could hardly sleep the night before, anticipating having to give hardline feedback, being confrontational, and communicating to Jacquie that we would be assuming the responsibility of paying back to the benefactor all wages paid to her.

In short, we were very upset, disappointed, embarrassed, and shocked. We believed we had been essentially dropped. This had turned out all backwards. Not only were we not any closer to our dream of expansion in the UK, but in fact we had contracted, given the loss of credibility in the eyes of our benefactor and now the possibility of losing Jacquie entirely and Liverpool along with her.

This felt a bit like ending a marriage and still having to live together. I had to teach the workshop. Jacquie had to assist. We had to be together for this weekend. Neither of us was looking forward to it.

I asked Jacquie an hour before the workshop to meet up. We pulled up two chairs. That we were able to meet and pull up two chairs was a testament to both sides in their commitment to taking the first step of containing the anxiety. There could easily have been many opportunities to triangle, gossip, establish camps, or gather more evidence. We had to sit in our anxiety, which was not easy. Containment is essential in order to find our way to the next step, which is to reflect rather than reload. Most people in situations involving high or even moderate anxiety do not contain and thus do not reflect, but simply go straight from trigger to reload.

I hadn't yet legitimately reflected so much as contained. I stared at Jacquie in silence, allowing my feelings to emerge. With tears in my eyes, I opened with telling Jacquie that the most important piece in all that had gone down was my concern for my relationship with her. I told her how important she was to me and that the loss of what had transpired as a company paled in comparison to my fear of the loss of our relationship. This wasn't about making someone wrong. This was more about sadness, loss, and tender, hurting feelings. I went on to report my personal history of fearing I didn't matter and being ultimately alone. In the end I was brave enough to ask, "What about our relationship, Jacquie? What about our relationship?"

This reflection and communication was me then doing 100% of my 50% of this relationship. I took ownership of my own anxiety and where it comes from in me, and communicated what my heart needed to say without concluding with any sense of good guys or bad guys, villains or victims. It was open. It felt risky. It was essential.

As I broke, so did Jacquie. Jacquie's personal history would tell her that she also didn't belong, was evil and an outcast. She had a long list of memories that suggested that once she made a mistake she was to be condemned. She went on to say that she didn't believe that she was worthy of a relationship and feared she should just go away as the ultimate correction. This fear had led to her not communicating, particularly about the relationship difficulties she was facing.

She had also contained and quietly supported Clearmind behind the scenes. Her love for Clearmind and our relationship had a strong pulse underneath the mutual distancing, projection, and avoidance.

By containing, reflecting rather than reloading, doing 100% or our 50%, and ultimately asking for help with the beliefs about self, we were then actually able to talk about the current issue with Clearmind UK going forward. And we did.

Both Jacquie and Duane took responsibility for their past beliefs, which were longing to completely cloud the present situation, and committed to considering self and other equally as the driving force in this predicament. They looked to the future and agreed to work together to forward all financial profits from future workshops, from both sides, to mutually pay the debt off. Many issues that had to be resolved were resolved. Relationships with each other became the most important consideration. Within minutes, what had initially presented as a lose-lose-lose moment became win-win-win.

Fast-forwarding to the present, Clearmind has expanded to several other UK cities, the debt has been paid off, and more importantly, all involved support and love each other.

SELF-APPLICATION: PERSONAL INVENTORY

Being emotionally responsible means being accountable. Take some time to do a personal inventory of people you have hurt when you have been operating from defence. Choose one or two who you will be accountable to by apologizing. Consider doing this in writing; sometimes people have an easier time absorbing information by reading it, as it alleviates any pressure to provide an immediate response. If this feels good, consider working your way through the whole list.

6 EVOLUTION THROUGH CONNECTION

"The law of evolution is that the strongest survives!"
"Yes, and the strongest, in the existence of any social species,
are those who are most social. In human terms, most
ethical. ... There is no strength to be gained from hurting
one another. Only weakness."
—Ursula K. Le Guin

We took a very long time to decide to write a book, in part because we fundamentally believe that the problems we experience started in relationships and therefore must be resolved in relationships as well. Connection is required for correction. There are many brilliant books out there that inspire people to more deeply understand themselves and change their minds. Connection is what allows us to change how we feel so that what we know, cognitively, to be true matches how we feel. How can we help people to do that in a therapeutically responsible way through a medium that is inherently a solo cognitive experience?

As we have seen, we are suffering not so much from the

traumatic or difficult events that we have experienced, we are suffering because of the meaning we have attached to these events. As long as we are holding on to this painful and inaccurate version of past events, we will keep running into it: we cannot disconnect from the story of our lives, because our stories inform who we are. We are not here to get rid of the past in order to become present, we are here to change our version of the past so that we can become present. Correction requires seeing not just self differently but expanding our view of all of the others who were involved in the story of our lives.

> Correction requires seeing not just self differently but expanding our view of all of the others who were involved in the story of our lives.

Attack and blame is projected guilt and shame. The degree to which someone is acting out and attacking is the degree to which they hate themselves. This very probably will not be apparent to one watching the behaviour, and very well might not be apparent to the one doing the behaviour, but it is nonetheless true. People don't choose to do horrific things just because. They do so because they are hurting. Paraphrasing *A Course in Miracles*, all behaviour is an extension of love or a call for it.

Being able to see that call for love, even if hidden under completely unacceptable behaviour, changes how you feel and allows for an opening to forgiveness. It creates soft, tender edges around even harsh stories and allows us to own them rather than feeling ashamed of them. This doesn't mean that harmful behaviour is okay, but being able to see the person underneath the hurtful behaviour makes all the difference, both in terms of how you respond in the present and the story you carry from the past. It is as important as having a new view of yourself.

Our introductory workshop culminates in an exercise called a re-enactment, which is essentially a trip to the basement, to the original scene of the crime, so to speak. After we have established connection, trust, and safety among our group members, we break off into smaller groups, under the direction of trained assistants, to role-play an event from their childhood where they know they took on an SOS and decided they had to construct a defence system.

In their small groups, each participant outlines the basic elements of what happened and assigns roles. They then play out the scene up to the point where they "split off" or shut down, and instead of shutting down, they are encouraged to express, uncensored, the feelings that they were not able to express at the time. Depending on the scene, this might start with upset or anger, but regardless of where it starts, it always drops to the pain and vulnerability underneath. The person in the basement is revealed.

The person in the basement is encouraged to express whatever they need to, including what they believe about self, others, and the world as a result of that experience. They hear from important others in the scene, from a place of vulnerability and ownership. How this happens varies, as each person and story is unique and requires a sensitive and unique approach. We don't change the story, we change the context and experience of the story, so that the participant emerges from the basement with a new sense of self, others, and the world.

Time and again we have been privileged to see the beauty of people when they are at their most vulnerable. It is ironic, but even when a person is confessing their fears about being not good enough, about being unlovable or flawed, it is evident to everyone else how beautiful, innocent, and pristine they actually are. It is as if the person we locked in the basement, revealed in this way, is actually unscathed and undamaged, no matter what might have happened in the past. The person in the basement emerges, in a way, as whole and complete as they were before being locked in.

It is this very human experience, more than any other, that informs our belief in the friendly universe. Human beings are far more than the sum of their life experiences, and there is a power in connection that transcends our individual natures. That experience of loving connection is what we would call "spiritual" or "God." There is tremendous power in a group of people connected through care and compassion in this way. Something becomes more important than our separate interests.

The re-enactment is a powerful transformative exercise, which we undertake with all the appropriate therapeutic cautions and safeguards. It is not an appropriate exercise to embark on without a skilled facilitator. The experience our participants have in this exercise is what we aspire to replicate here to some degree in order to make this book what we wish it to be. Transformation requires opening up the basement in the presence of a safe, loving other person, allowing uncensored emotional expression, and moving through to correction of the mistaken beliefs that are at the root of our suffering.

To that end, we are going to introduce you to the 4-Step Getting Real Process, which we typically teach in our workshops as a maintenance tool for our participants to use when they return home, to the real workshop. The four-step process is a structure that will help you get in touch with what you are holding in your basement, in order to connect and correct those mistaken beliefs. It is designed to be used with a current upset and to use that upset to trace what has been triggered in your basement. You can also start with the basement, meaning use it as a way of working through those past scenes directly. Particularly if you have not done one of our workshops, we ask you to attend to the following cautions:

1. This is a process done with a partner. Pick someone you trust, someone who has also read this book. Read through the process a few times before you give it a try. Ideally, it is great to have a third person who has studied the process to coach the reporter and witness through it. You can change roles and take turns doing the process (being the reporter).

2. Practise, and follow the structure strictly. The structure will feel stilted at first because you are having to think and feel at the same time. Once you become familiar with the structure, the process will flow easily. Practise about less upsetting or inflamed issues at first, again so that you get used to the process.

3. As with any aspect of this book, if something gets stirred up in you that feels overwhelming, consider seeking professional help to work your way through it, either through workshops such as ours, run by qualified professionals, or with the help of a therapist trained in relational/experiential therapies.

THE 4-STEP GETTING REAL PROCESS

Having come this far in the book, we now know that managing our anxiety by acting out or in simply brings back to us the very upset we hoped acting in or out would get rid of. Committing instead to containing that anxiety, reflecting rather than reloading, and communicating vulnerably is not only a better way to go, but the only way to go. We outlined how to reconcile the difference between asking for help and asking for rescue. In many instances asking for help will require the assistance of a qualified therapist who understands this type of approach, or attending one of our workshops to be guided through by a trained facilitator.

Short of that, the 4-Step Getting Real Process provides a therapeutic structure that is very effective in walking us through. It is like having a free therapist, provided you strictly remain within the guidelines and structure. As stated above, our recommendation initially is to only address issues in your life that are not more than you can handle once opened up. We suggest you start by practising with upsets that would be considered minor and not highly anxious situations or traumas, until you feel safe, comfortable, supported, and more familiar with the process.

Whenever we experience emotional distress in relationship, whether with a primary relationship partner or anyone else, we are being gifted with an opportunity. Any degree of upset, whether it be a twinge of uneasiness or a full-blown hysterical fit, is always an indicator that some fear-based belief from the past has been activated in the present. This process is a tool that allows you to use upset as a window to the past in order to correct the SOS (suspicion of self) held there.

The 4-Step Getting Real Process requires the participation of two people. The roles of each are clearly defined: one will be the reporter, the active participant, and the other, the witness. The witness is there to stand in for anyone you might be upset with in the present or past. The process can be done with any willing partner, someone who has also studied the process we are about to outline. Each of you will take turns going through the process, so each will have the opportunity to be a reporter and a witness.

We do use the 4-Step Process as a tool for couples to work through their upsets together; it has tremendous connective power for couples. However, it takes a lot of practice and containment skill on the part of the witness to do this, as the first step in particular is uncensored expression about the upset. Because we are introducing this process in a book format, we are recommending against doing it with the person you are upset with. Instead, you can bring your vulnerable self to the person after you work through the process (meaning Steps 2–4).

In most other therapeutic conflict-resolution schemes, dialogue is encouraged because issues are typically viewed as a "communication problem." Despite this book being all about connection, you may be surprised to hear that during times of conflict we strongly discourage conversation.

When times are tense between two people, it is so easy to give in to the temptation to get rid of the battleground inside of self (the basement) by dumping it out and having the battleground in the relationship instead. For example, if you open up the issue and the other argues, agrees, or tries to fix it in reaction, the battleground now is outside of self, between you. When we succeed in transferring blame onto him or her or this or that, we have avoided addressing our deeper fears about self.

Many relationships exist this way for decades, with both keeping the relationship as the battleground by keeping the fight going with endless arguments and issues. As uncomfortable as it is, the function of the dysfunction is that it is a way of avoiding self by making the problem in the other. As we have seen, we actually amplify our pain when we engage in this defence. The only way through is through the basement.

This process is more of a monologue than a dialogue for that reason. The process is designed to have the one upset express and the witness let it bounce off like a mirror and, in a sense, return to the one trying to get rid of it, so that the battleground remains where the battleground actually is: in self. Healing is impossible until it does.

Some people are more able to access self-attacking thoughts than they are able to access other-attacking thoughts. It is fine to use this process to work through self-attack or upset at self in the same way as you would use it to work through upset at another person.

THE REPORTER

The ultimate task of the reporter is to remain willing: willing to ultimately take complete responsibility for their own experience and willing to see things differently. This can be challenging, since getting real involves the active discharge (through open one-way communication) of intense feeling. Everything has to get onto the table. When we become upset about something, our strategic self screams that someone or something must be to blame. Going into the process, you have to be willing to be wrong. It doesn't mean you are wrong, but you have to be willing to be.

One of the most difficult tasks for the reporter is to be scrupulously honest, willing to explore and report all the dark corners of the activity of the strategic self. You have to be willing to be where you are before you can get to where you want to go. That means reporting where you are instead of hiding. This uncensored communication often runs contrary to all we have practised in the past.

Some people can easily access their anger, which is where the process begins, but some relate more easily to the term "upset." Either is okay, and in fact, it is okay to start with exactly where you are, whatever the emotional experience. The task is simply to report honestly rather than hide. If you allow yourself to express the upset, it will reveal the vulnerability hiding underneath, which is where we are aiming. Please note that "uncensored communication" means full expression of feeling, not name-calling.

It can be just as difficult to express honestly from the tender feelings in the basement, but it is so important to do so. Self-attack is not vulnerability: if you are feeling angry at yourself, that expression belongs in the first step of the process. The degree to which you allow yourself to feel and express from the person in the basement without allowing your thoughts to inhibit the process equals the degree to which you will feel the correction on the other side. Feeling good requires allowing feelings.

Above all, remain determined to take responsibility for the strategic self's fear-based projections. As reporters, we need to remain solid in our commitment to our own healing, which requires taking complete ownership of our experience.

THE WITNESS

When faced with upset in the 4-Step Process, the task for the witness is to remain absolutely neutral, to contain and not take on the projections. The job of the witness is to "mind the store" for the truth by remembering the essence of who the reporter is beyond the presenting upset, no matter how convincing. The witness does this without responding in any way outside the prescribed parameters.

By refusing to buy into the other person's projections by agreeing, arguing, or fixing, the witness allows the other the space necessary to heal their pained mind. The battleground remains within the reporter, where it can be transformed, rather than anchoring itself in the relationship. Sometimes it is helpful to literally visualize a mirror in front of you, facing the reporter, from which the reporter's communications bounce off, returning to their place of origin.

Now, in the strictest terms, the witness is only to say the words prescribed in the process, but given that we have specified that the witness is *not* the one you are upset with, they may provide some coaching through the process if necessary by reminding you of the words, or asking "Just like when?" at the appropriate time.

BEGINNING THE PROCESS: THE PRAYER

Intention is everything. Initiating the Getting Real Process is a statement of willingness to release the need to be right and in control, in favour of the goal of finding happiness and peace, thus relinquishing control to a friendly universe. All that is asked is a little bit of willingness to do so, but that little bit is essential to the process.

As a demonstration of that little bit of willingness, a simple prayer is said prior to the 4-Step. Whenever two meet to get real, these are the words to be concurrently spoken while looking into the other's eyes: "I commit to seeing you, me, and everyone else as innocent, in order to return to a state of love and peace." This statement means that I am committed to seeing innocence in myself and in you, to seeing the love and call for love underneath every behaviour, because in seeing the truth about self and the world, I will find peace.

If the reporter has no willingness to see the situation any other way than through eyes of judgement and attack, the process should be delayed until such time as that willingness is offered.

PART A: UNCENSORED EXPRESSION

In order for this process to work, it is essential to connect deeply to the emotional, feeling state. Part A is entirely focused on expanding the reporter's direct experience of feeling. It is intended to get the reporter completely out of analysis, or the head, and into the emotions, eventually to contact the heart. The reporter should speak as if this is all happening now rather than then, to make it more immediate. Again, this is expression of feeling, not name-calling.

You can pick a current situation or person you are upset with or a past one to work with. You can choose to attack yourself if that is the only way you access anger. No matter how you begin, the process will lead to the past.

Step 1: Expressing the upset
In Step 1, the reporter gives full, authentic expression to the angry, attacking level of consciousness. The reporter shares uncensored their current upset state, withheld thoughts, and judgements and conflicts related to self and the other. The reporter makes one simple, short statement at a time, beginning with "What I want you to hear is I am angry (or frustrated)…," "What I want you to hear is I hate it when you…," or "What I want you to hear is I'm upset that…" Again, if the reporter is speaking from memories, they should speak as if this is all happening now rather than then, to make it more immediate and real. No name-calling, that is, you would not say "What I want you to hear is you are a
_____."

The witness responds to each short statement with "I hear you."

The reporter: What I want you to hear is [I am angry that you were late again last night].
The witness: I hear you.
The reporter: What I want you to hear is [I'm upset that you don't spend time with me].
The witness: I hear you.

To the extent that the reporter can fully express their upset mind in Step 1, they will also be able to open up to heal the guilt- and shame-based mind that their defence protects. When reporting your upset/attack thoughts, you may also include your upset/attack on self. For example, "What I want you to hear is I hate that I am so needy."

There are also a few points to make here about technique. Statements should always be directed at the person they pertain to, in a way that lets the witness stand in for whomever you are expressing to in the moment. For example, if the witness is standing in for the person you are upset with, you would still say, "Karen, I am angry at you…," rather than "I am angry at Karen…" as if that person were sitting there. Keeping statements directed in this way helps to expand immediate experience. Do your best to avoid long pauses between statements, as these are an indication of censoring, deleting, or minimizing.

We allow a maximum of five minutes for this part of the process.

Here are some anger and attack words to help you label and express your feelings for Step 1: angry, annoyed, disgusted, enraged, frustrated, hate, irritated, judge, mad, suspicious, upset, aggravated, exasperated, irked, enraged, furious, incensed, irate, livid, outraged, resentful, appalled, hostile, repulsed, horrified, agitated, disturbed, perturbed, shocked, wary, mistrustful, displeased.

Step 2: Contacting the vulnerable self
When the upset expression has been exhausted and has no interference other than the response of "I hear you," there is a natural drop into the vulnerable self beneath the defence. Here we contact root feelings of fear, sadness, loneliness, shame, hurt, and so on. Although we can feel anger, anger is not what we term a root feeling, in that it is always masking or guarding a deeper sense of loss. It is a defence, despite its emotional intensity. We are aiming for what the guard is guarding.

Some root-feeling words in the family of fear include frightened, scared, terrified, afraid, dread, panicked, petrified, anxious, overwhelmed, tense, nervous, stressed out, jittery, turmoil, rattled, distressed, worried.

Root feelings in the realm of vulnerability and loss include sad, despair, depressed, despondent, anguished, devastated, grief, heartbroken, bereaved, hurt, lonely, miserable, hopeless, unhappy, ashamed, embarrassed, guilty, mortified, vulnerable, fragile, helpless, insecure, sensitive, hurt, lost, devastated, forlorn, self-conscious.

In Step 2, then, the reporter's job is to expose and give voice to the vulnerable self by contacting the underlying root feeling. At this point, the reporter should only be in touch with root feelings; if anger comes up, Step 1 has not been completed. This is the beginning of the reporter taking ownership of their experience.

Attack thoughts are about other; root feelings will be a communication about self. For example, saying "I feel lonely" is different than saying "You don't seem to want me." It is important to note that the vulnerable state is a visceral one that is not cognitive. Sad, scared, alone, and desperate are all vulnerable words and are not interpretive or analytical. These feelings are the gateway to your SOS, which is identified in Step 3—but we are not all the way there yet. In Step 2, we are now emotionally naked, without protection or analysis.

The witness receives the communication from the vulnerable self by responding, "I hear you" and invites more communication, adding, "Is there more?"

When it is apparent that the vulnerable self is present, it is time for the reporter to add the second part: "just like when…" We use the root feeling as a window to trace back into the past the point at which the reporter can first remember feeling the same way. Depending on how much the reporter is allowing their emotional experience, the past scene may occur right away or it may occur after several statements describing the facets of the root feeling.

> The reporter: Underneath my attack, I really feel [scared].
> The witness: I hear you. Is there more?
> The reporter: Underneath my attack, I really feel [sad].
> The witness: I hear you. Is there more?
> The reporter: Underneath my attack, I really feel [lonely],
> just like when [my dad left when I was six].
> The witness: I hear you. Is there more?

Once we reach this level, it is impossible not to immediately redefine the source of the problem. At this point, the witness should be feeling some relief, having seen the vulnerability underlying the defence, having widened the scope of the history of this feeling. We may have even arrived at the original psychological scene of the crime from the past that is being projected on the present. The shift in redefining the problem from "out there" to "in here" has a tremendous impact.

PART B: RETURNING TO LOVE

Part B of the process is focused on correction, on uncovering and correcting mistaken beliefs.

Step 3: Revealing the suspicion of self, other, and world

Root feelings are the visceral state that result from our SOS. We have the experience of fear when we do not believe we are good enough, worthy enough, loveable, and so on. Now that we have arrived at the scene of the crime in the past, it is possible to uncover the suspicion of self and the mistaken beliefs that resulted. We have amplified the root feeling by focusing on revealing it, and the past scene connected to the feeling, and now we can use the root feeling as a conduit to the suspicion of self, other, and world.

This step might at first be experienced as confusing or difficult, but it is also the most important step of all. This step has the reporter taking responsibility for what they have been up to. Essentially, the reporter is admitting that the focus on the current issue is being used to prove a longstanding suspicion of self, other, and the world. We are admitting that the belief that "I am not good enough" didn't start because of what the other is doing to us. That we are using our perception of what the other is doing to prove our lifelong belief that we are not good enough.

In many ways, our strategies are perpetually on the lookout, searching for every scrap of evidence they can to reinforce the longstanding notion of the our SOS. In difficult or charged moments of our lives, we are not so much perceiving reality as we are seeking to prove our SOS. "See, I knew it," we say to ourselves. What we "know" comes from the basement, and instead of being at the mercy of external circumstances, we are actually screening out important aspects of what is happening, or what did happen, to prove our fears. This step ought to feel like a confession, having the complete absence of any sense of good guys and bad guys, or "whodunit." This includes the past as well as the present.

If this point remains confusing, please read again. It is critically important that this step be understood, not just for improving the success of the process, but to truly understand the magnitude of what it means to formally re-identify the problem from him or her or this or that to the real battleground in self, with the meanings we attached to events and continue to try to prove.

Here the reporter simply keys into the mistaken beliefs, the SOS, and is admitting the intention of trying to prove them to be true. The reporter starts this step off with the words "What I want you to hear is I have been trying to prove my fear that (I am, you are, life is…)" followed by a pause, a moment of reflection, and then the words that invite correction to occur: "But I have been mistaken." The witness continues to respond in the prescribed manner.

> The reporter: I want you to hear that I have been trying to prove my fear [that I cannot trust], but I have been mistaken.
> The witness: I hear you. Is there more?
> The reporter: I want you to hear that I have been trying to prove my fear [that I am not good enough and that is why my dad left], but I have been mistaken.

The witness: I hear you. Is there more?

The reporter: I want you to hear that I have been trying to prove my fear [that I'm not loveable], but I have been mistaken.

The witness: I hear you. Is there more?

The reporter: I want you to hear that I have been trying to prove my fear [that the universe must be an unfriendly place and I should be on guard all the time], but I have been mistaken.

The witness: I hear you. Is there more?

It is very important to note here that we are uncovering beliefs and beliefs only: we are not referring to behaviours or situations. For example, you could not say "I want you to hear that I have been trying to prove my fear that you will leave me, but I have been mistaken." The other might leave. If you find yourself diverted into behaviours rather than beliefs, ask yourself, "What would it mean if that did happen?" For example, "What would it mean if you left me? Oh, that I'm not good enough."

The reason for focusing on beliefs is simple. Our beliefs determine our experience to a very large degree. We have limited control over the events of our lives and less control over the actions of others. We do, however, have complete control over what we choose to believe about these events or behaviours, and what we choose to believe will make the difference between a fearful, painful existence and a peaceful one.

The steps, particularly this one, may feel technical at first. However, if you understand the intention and concept behind it, the step tends to flow more easily. To summarize this step, if it were in fact a conversation it would sound something like this: "You know, when you walked out the door I jumped all over it...like a vulture. Sorry about that. Actually, I have to confess that I am using you walking out the door to prove that I must not be loveable at all. It's hard for me to admit that. Really hard. In fact, my fear is that I have never been loveable, ever since my dad left when I was six. How crazy is that, to make that my fault as a six-year-old? What did I know? ... I think I've had it wrong all along."

STEP 4: CORRECTION THROUGH CONNECTION

This final step of the process is integrating this new understanding and asking for help. It is here that the reporter connects with the witness from the level of suspicion of self, other, and world, in order to correct it and return to the real world, which will have much more to do with love than defence and strategy. Ultimately, we are here to heal our belief in separation, and the most efficient way to do so is by legitimately connecting and legitimately asking for help. We didn't get into this mess alone and we can't get out that way, either.

In this last portion of "getting real," we are getting real in the sense of returning to a closer sense of reality, the truth of the friendly universe that exists beyond our mistaken perceptions of it, and the undamaged self that continues to exist exactly where we left it, as beautiful and pristine. The friendly universe exists at another order of reality, strictly at the level of knowledge of and faith in its inherent friendliness, which is not attached to specific events, behaviours, or outcomes. Thus, we cannot say "Help me to remember that you will never leave me," because physical, worldly events are unpredictable. Instead, we would say "Help me to remember that even if you did leave me, I am okay and worthy, and am never alone." "Help me to remember that you have the right to choose how to live your life, which is not a comment on my value or worth."

The reporter corrects the suspicion of self, other, and world in this step, and the witness reflects back that reality by repeating it back to the reporter. Because it is so vitally important that the reporter actually be willing to believe this correction, we then add a step where the witness asks the reporter if they accept the truth.

> The reporter: Please help me to transform the belief that
> [I am not good enough] and remember the
> truth [that I am good enough, no matter
> what anyone else says or does].
> The witness: I will help you to remember the truth [that
> you are good enough, no matter what
> anyone else says or does]. Do you accept
> [that you are good enough]?
> The reporter: I accept (or don't) [that I am good enough].

> The reporter: Please help me to transform the belief that
> [I can't trust] and remember the truth [that
> I can trust in a friendly universe, that there
> is always something good in every situation].
> The witness: I will help you remember the truth [that
> you can trust in a friendly universe,
> that there is always something good in every
> situation]. Do you accept [that you can trust
> in a friendly universe]?
> The reporter: I accept (or don't) [that I can trust in a
> friendly universe].

When the reporter accepts the correction, honesty is essential. If you as the reporter really are not willing to accept the correction, then say so specifically, for example, "I don't accept that I can trust." Authenticity and ownership of the problem is a major component that is vital to the success of this exercise, so even if you find yourself completely unwilling to accept a correction, owning that this is your choice and yours alone is accountable, and redefines the problem. You will find that owning your belief in this way exaggerates your dilemma, and you may find yourself more willing to revisit the problematic belief again later in the process, and choose again.

It is important to note here that the correction "remembering..." is always framed in positive language, never negative. Our brains respond to positive language and actually don't have the immediate ability to hear negative language. For example, if I said, "Don't think about a green elephant," what do you think about? Thus, when giving voice to a correction, you would not say "Help me to remember that I am not guilty"; you would say instead, "Help me to remember that I am innocent."

Maintaining eye contact with the witness is also critical. Whenever we look down, we are losing contact with the present and returning to the past. Staying focused in the here and now will help cement the corrected belief into consciousness.

The 4-Step Getting Real Process in Brief

Use this short form for reference as you practise.

Stating the intention

Looking into each other's eyes, each says in turn: *I commit to seeing you, me, and everyone as innocent, in order to return to a state of love and peace.*

Step 1 (5 min.): Attack and blame

(finger is metaphorically pointed out, at them)

The reporter: *I want you to hear that...* [attack/upset is expressed, e.g., I'm angry that you were late again last night].

The reporter reports uncensored upset, one short statement at a time, beginning with "I want you to hear that..." followed by upset, e.g., "I am angry (upset, resentful, frustrated)..., I hate it..., I judge..."

The witness: *I hear you.*

The witness receives the reporter's communication as neutrally as possible.

Step 2 (10 min.): Contacting the vulnerable self

The reporter: *I want you to hear that underneath my attack, I really feel...* [root feeling, e.g., scared and lonely], *just like when...* [past scene, e.g., my dad left when I was six].

The reporter reports the feeling under the anger (guilty, sad, scared, lonely, hurt, ashamed, terrified, vulnerable, etc.) and identifies the first time in their life they remember feeling that way. This should feel like a confession as opposed to a continued focusing on other to explain the pain.

The witness: *I hear you. Is there more?*

The witness receives the reporter's communication as neutrally as possible and invites more communication from the level of vulnerability.

Step 3 (5 min.): Revealing the suspicion of self/other/world
(finger is turned inward, at self)

The reporter: *I want you to hear that I have been trying to prove my fear that...* [suspicion of self/other/world, e.g., that I am not good enough] *...but I have been mistaken.*

The reporter traces the mistaken belief (not behaviour) about self/other/world emerging from the past.

The witness: *I hear you. Is there more?*

Step 4 (5 min.): Correction through connection

The reporter: *Will you help me to transform the belief that...* [suspicion of self/other/world, e.g., I am not good enough] *and remember the truth...* [reality belief, e.g., that I am good enough, no matter what anyone else says or does].

The reporter identifies the suspicion of self/other/world being projected from the past and asks for help to remember the reality that underlies events and behaviours. Remember to correct attacking beliefs about others mentioned in the first step.

The witness: *I will help you to remember the truth...* [reality belief, e.g., that you are good enough, no matter what anyone else says or does]. *Do you accept...* [reality belief, e.g., that you are good enough]?

The witness receives the request and reflects back the corrected belief only, as accurately as possible, with no adding, interpreting, or deleting. The witness asks for confirmation that the reporter is willing to accept the correction.

The reporter: *I accept (or don't)…* [reality belief, e.g., that I am good enough].

The reporter accepts (or doesn't) the corrected belief, based on a reality that underlies events or behaviours. If the reporter is unable to accept, they have the option to repeat this portion again.

7 GETTING REAL IN REAL LIFE

We have a saying here in India. Everything will be all right in the end... If it's not all right, then it's not yet the end.
—**Sonny, in the movie** *The Best Exotic Marigold Hotel*

FARMER PARABLE: WHO KNOWS IF IT IS GOOD OR BAD?

Once there was a farmer who worked his poor farm, together with his son and their one horse. During a storm one night, the wind blew down the small corral and their horse ran off scared into the hills. Their neighbour came over to say, "Such bad luck, you've lost your only horse. How are you going to work your fields?" The farmer stayed calm and replied, "Who knows if it is good or bad?"

The next day, the horse returned from the hills with two wild horses in tow. The farmer and his son quickly reassembled the corral and secured all three horses inside. The neighbour returned, exclaiming, "Such good luck, you now have three horses!" The farmer smiled and said, "Who knows if it is good or bad?"

Shortly after, the farmer's son, in an attempt to tame the

horses, was thrown and broke his leg. Again the neighbour ran over. "Such bad, bad luck! How sad for you!" The farmer again looked intently at the neighbour and calmly said, "Who knows if it is good or bad?"

Later on, a neighbouring army was threatening the farmer's village. With the local soldiers marching down the rural roads conscripting young men to the army to fight the invaders, they came across the son, who had broken his leg, and left him behind. The neighbour returned, jubilant that the farmer's son had been spared from fighting, claiming good luck had once again taken place. "Who knows if it is good or bad?" was all that the farmer said.

This parable speaks to difficulties similar to those we encounter all day long. One part (the neighbour) is hanging on to a narrow view, and the other (the farmer) is open and curious. The neighbour is closed to any new information beyond what is known, and the farmer is open and unwilling to come to conclusions, being governed by the mystery of the unknown.

The meaning any situation or experience has is the meaning we give it. The habitual known meaning we give it gets recycled from our past. We only see what we are looking for; in a state of anxiety, we see what we fear. We paste our unresolved experiences and conclusions from the past all over the face of the present. How little does it take for this to happen? How quickly do we conclude and react?

When the anxiety is high, we must humbly admit that we are more in relationship with our version of the past than with the present. We are more in relationship with who is not there now than with who is there now. Depending on the level of anxiety lying dormant from our past, we may have absolutely no accurate perception of the person or situation in front of us that has triggered that anxiety.

The moment we conclude, we reach the end of the story, just as the story is actually beginning. The situation itself has infinite meaning and possibility, but we mostly settle for what we make it mean, which is what we already know. If it is an anxious situation, as is the case with the farmer story, the neighbour's anxiety is dictating what he fears it must mean or what he wishes it to mean. Both of these opposite conclusions (good luck, bad luck) are based on his own prior learning. They are conceived of as either a continuation of his past experience (bad luck) or an answer to it (good luck). He is projecting rather than perceiving reality. Further, he requires very little to reach his predictable conclusions and be essentially oblivious to what is actually taking place in front of him. He spends most of his days, as many of us do, never being curious about any deeper meaning or possibility.

> The moment we conclude, we reach the end of the story, just as the story is actually beginning.

The farmer, on the other hand, subscribes to the notion that ultimately we never know what anything means because life is in a constant process of change. We can choose to relate to the unknown as the mysterious unveiling of the friendliness of the universe, with its own ups and downs, moving along and evolving. The farmer and the neighbour are both witnessing and giving meaning to what is occurring in front of them consistent with the frame or context that they are bringing to it. The meaning they give it says much more about what is taking place inside of them than what is taking place in front of them.

Context determines meaning: Projection vs. perception

From the figure above, what do you see? Is the centre figure 13 or B? Or is it both? What you see is not only up to you but, more importantly, about you. The meaning is determined by the context or frame of reference you are using. If I came from the planet Numbers, I would find the numerical meaning and see 13; if my history was from the planet Alphabet, I would attribute an alphabetical meaning to the same centre figure and see B.

We are all very much involved in what we see. If the neighbour had a history of loss, abuse, and disappointment, it would follow that he would file the experience of the horse running into the hills as evidence of bad luck. Conversely, if the farmer had a personal story of experiencing trust and good endings to even bad stories, he would see that the horse running to the hills was not the end of the story, just a chapter. There is more to come. The farmer would hold the experience in the context of "hanging in there": there is more to come even with the positive experiences.

We were walking down a trail by the river near our home, which is on the rainy west coast of Canada. It was a beautiful, sunny day. We passed a man on the trail, and Duane said, "Beautiful day, isn't it?" The man responded, "Yeah, but it's not going to last!" Factually speaking, both were correct. Both responses also reveal how our beliefs act as filters for our perception. We see what we are looking for.

If, for example, a person has a pervasive SOS of being not good enough, the world outside of self would be perceived as one of ever-looming judgement and attack, regardless of what was actually taking place. Our evaluation of self strongly influences what we witness in front of us. Perception is not so much a window through which we perceive an objective view of reality as a mirror reflecting back to us the self we are either celebrating, accepting, or in judgement of.

The cost of believing and running with the meaning we give our experiences is enormous. The moment the anxiety rises, the conclusion we make and the decision to not look beyond what we think we know prevents us from experiencing anything new. New information is vital to our personal evolution. Each and every difficult, anxiety-producing experience holds the possibility of entering the unknown, where we discover new territory instead of revisiting old territory.

OPEN THE DOOR TO THE BASEMENT AND STEP ONTO THE PLAYING FIELD

Practising the five skills of emotional responsibility with consistency will allow us to emerge out of the bondage of our past. We must be willing to face our own anxiety and no longer be so easily pushed around by it (containment, doing 100% of your 50%). We must become aware of what we are carrying in our basements from the past (reflect vs. reload). With this self-awareness, we can then open up to some long-overdue new information through connecting and correcting our SOSs (vulnerable communication, asking for help).

In our view, it takes only 15 minutes to change the course of your life. Not change your life, but change the course or direction. If you are facing the right direction, it doesn't matter how fast you are going. Something happens. Your partner might say, "We need to talk." Your boss raises his voice. You are stuck in traffic and are going to be late. Your hair is thinning. You have gained five pounds. Your daughter is ignoring you. A large surprise bill comes in the mail or your inbox. Your horse runs off into the hills!

When something happens, it is as though we become aware that there is something outside the comfort zone we naturally gravitate towards on the sidelines of life. We become aware that we have a basement; there is a knock on the door. The knock catalyzes historic beliefs, sounding off alarm bells and anxiety. Anxiety tells us to fight, flee, or freeze. We are convinced the knock on the basement door is the precursor to every horror movie we've ever watched. The door is saturated with what we fear to be true: a compilation of handed-down beliefs, memories, rules, and views on self, life, and relationships that all add up to some kind of danger. "Do not enter!" the strategic mind hollers. And we listen. We turn to our strategies.

Fifteen minutes of containing that anxiety and reflecting may be 15 minutes longer than you or any member of your family system have ever legitimately taken. The anxiety is so perpetual and chronic, and the family rules and patterns meant to deal with it so engrained, that we may simply not have any idea that there is possibility beyond what we think we already know. A lifetime can go by without any significant reflection, and the baton is then passed to the next generation to figure it all out.

Every day, new situations, new people, and events from outside come knocking on our basement door. Because we are certain of what is about to happen, we rarely take any steps through that door to challenge that fear and discover the truth. As we have seen, our choice to hide, pretend, and defend amplifies what we have locked in our basement. We inevitably fall to what we believe is our fate, remaining there rather than rising to our destiny on the other side.

The movie *Groundhog Day* may be a perfect example of this process. There is Phil the weatherman, sentenced (in his mind) to cover Groundhog Day in Punxsutawney each year. He dreads it, resents it, and views it as an insult that takes him off his course of becoming a famous anchorman on the nightly news. He gets caught in the twilight zone loop of re-experiencing the same day over and over again, meeting the same boring hostess in his hotel, the old high school nerd on the street, and the aggravating news crew, including his eventual love interest, the producer. These people are all perceived to be the obstacles in his way to the fame he longs for and, in his mind, so deserves.

The premise of the movie is that, over and over, Phil wakes up to experience the exact same day: Groundhog Day in Punxsutawney. After testing many strategic personalities to get the most of these repetitive days (including money and sex), Phil collapses and finally gives up. He has his 15 minutes of containment. He reflects and begins to appreciate how selfish and cruel he has been. His heart opens when he attempts to save the life of a dying street person he previously never cared to notice, but fails. He puts his hand on the door and walks through. He realizes all of this hatred and condemnation for all those around him was just a projection of how much he hated himself. He enters the playing field with an open heart, despite how deeply hurting or scarred his heart is. It is a heart. It is vulnerable. It is feeling.

He stays on the playing field long enough to look around and notice more about these people and fellow crew members who he had previously thought were the problem. They transform from two-dimensional obstacles to three-dimensional people just like him. He gets to know them. He cares about them. He brings the crew coffee and doughnuts in the morning. He grieves the dying old man and hugs his old nerdy high school acquaintance. He falls in love. He discovers on the playing field that those he previously perceived as being in the way were, in fact, the way.

Our lives have an intrinsic impulse towards evolution. In order to evolve, we must be willing to face our anxiety and sit in and contain the anxiety long enough to move towards vulnerability and emotional responsibility instead of defence and strategy. Contain. Fifteen minutes. Reflect rather than reload. We do not know what is about to happen. We only think we do.

A brave new world waits on the other side of the basement door. It's been waiting there a long time. Your parents stood where you are, and generations before that. You may be the first to return to what has been, historically, the battleground in your family system. It's time to put your hand on the door and turn the handle.

Fifteen minutes to stay looking at the door and asking yourself a very important question: is what I fear a certainty? How would I actually know? Where does this fear actually come from? With your hand on the door, you are already breaking all the rules. With your hand on the door and walking towards what you do not know rather than what you do, your life is about to change. You are about to enter the playing field where the perceived danger awaits. In order to enter your curiosity, your faith in the unknown must be greater than your long loyalty to what you think you know. Faith must override fear.

Even with the Do Not Enter lights flashing, this is also where healing begins. This is where you get to have a long-overdue meeting with yourself. This is where someone can actually meet you. Your task here now is to contain, reflect, step in, stay in, and take a look around. This is a time to measure your success by who you are becoming rather than by external outcome. Whether the relationship transforms before your eyes, or you receive the raise, is secondary to whether you are becoming more of who you authentically are. This is the real prize.

THE PLAYING FIELD: STEP IN, STAY IN, AND LOOK AROUND

The playing field is a metaphor for your relationship web, used for healing instead of harm. Your relationships will bring every opportunity that you need to evolve or stay stuck, and if you take the opportunities presented to practice your emotional responsibility skills, evolution is guaranteed. In the basement, we keep our fears alive by keeping real selves separate from our relationship web and engaging with our strategies and defence. We stay on the sidelines, thinking that safety is somehow going to result in happiness. The basement is only a basement when we hide, pretend, and defend.

When we choose to challenge our fears and show up in our relationships in an emotionally responsible way, we walk through the door to the basement and step onto the playing field. We discover the real, connected existence that is always available. Contain, reflect, and choose an emotionally responsible response: this is what it means to "step in."

> Your relationships will bring every opportunity that you need to evolve or stay stuck, and if you take the opportunities presented to practise your emotional responsibility skills, evolution is guaranteed.

"Stay in" means hang on to yourself, contain, do 100% of your 50%, and don't give in to the temptation to revert to your old beliefs and patterns. Don't revert to control strategies, thinking you need a certain outcome to be okay. Do what it takes to stay in authentic, vulnerable connection with the world around you.

Look around and deliberately open up to new evidence instead of trying to prove your fear. Take a new picture to replace the fear-based one you took long ago and continue to project. Step in, stay in, and look around.

Repeat all of the above as needed! We wish we could provide you with a nice, linear road map, but life doesn't work that way. Evolution is an ongoing and circular process, requiring you to constantly meet yourself and challenge your patterned ways of thinking, feeling, and behaving. To help better understand how this works, we will walk you through how this looks in action in intimate relationships with friends, family, and at work.

LIFE ON THE PLAYING FIELD: INTIMATE RELATIONSHIPS

There is no area in any person's life where the anxious alarm bells ring louder than in intimate relationships. In our primary relationships, so much is at stake. As the other becomes more and more important in your life, the strategic self becomes more and more alert, looking out for danger all the way from the living room to the bedroom. So much to lose but, here more than any other place, so much to gain.

Step in (It always starts with one person)
With Catherine and Duane, evolution began with her courageous words "If you say that one more time, I will believe you." Systemic change, meaning changing the pattern, always starts with one. One person has to step out of the dance and step in to the relationship with their real self. Catherine had one shivering hand on the door to her basement and one gently on Duane's as she proclaimed, "If you say that one more time, I will believe you," which, as we have seen, resulted from a period of containment and reflection. She was divorcing herself from outcome, not from Duane. She had no idea whether this relationship would make it or not, but she was issuing an invitation.

To legitimately reflect and walk through the basement door, letting go of a need for outcome is critical. The need for outcome is the drive inside us that got us into trouble in the first place: "I need this to be okay." Our strategies do not work; the only thing that can work is when we bring our real selves back into the real world. Whatever happens when you bring your real self, honestly and responsibly, has to be the right thing. Stepping in means being prepared to let go of who we think we need to be, meeting who we fear we are in the basement in order to finally discover who we truly are in authentic connection.

Catherine spoke the words (the result of containing and reflecting); once the words were spoken, she was on the playing field. This is similar to diving off the side of a pool deck. Once you leave the edge, there is no going back. She was on her way. She then left it with Duane. His 15 minutes of reflection actually required two days.

> When we drop our defences and let go of outcome, we are in a vulnerable state. It is raw and undefended. It is also beautiful and extremely attractive, because it is real.

When we drop our defences and let go of outcome, we are in a vulnerable state. It is raw and undefended. It is also beautiful and extremely attractive, because it is real. There is nothing more compelling than a person relinquishing the world and everyone in it of the responsibility for their emotional, psychological, or spiritual well-being. To stand on the playing field by first dropping our strategic masks, revealing and reconciling the SOS, and beginning the process of remembering the true self starts a process akin to a spiritual-evolutionary tsunami. It takes so little to generate so much.

Stay in
You have now stepped in. The task is now to stay in by doing 100% of your 50%, no more or less, and leaving the relationship with its own sense of urgency. This is a time for holding on to yourself and allowing the other to meet themselves...or not. Both will feel uncomfortable. The other actually has a right to their discomfort and pain: it is not kind to try to protect others from their own struggle, because that struggle is a necessary component of their evolution. Staying on the playing field means meeting a new level of anxiety and reflection. Can you respectfully leave the other to be with self as well?

It only takes one. As we mentioned earlier, it is important to measure the success of entering the playing field by who you are there rather than by the outcome. In some cases, the other may not participate—they may, in fact, turn up their strategic self to entice you back into yours. Hanging on to yourself through this difficult period is critical. Your task is to be, yourself, what you want the relationship to be, by being caring instead of caretaking, being available instead of over- or underfunctioning, being giving but not a doormat, being transparent but not invisible: doing 100% of your 50%. The other may not make the trip and may keep taking shots from their strategic self. There is no guarantee.

At the end of the day, if who you authentically are is not allowed into the relationship, you have to wonder what is going on. If the only part of you that is allowed entry into the relationship is your mask or strategies, you also have to ask yourself if you can actually lose what you never had. On the hopeful end of the spectrum, however, the probability of the relationship working is much greater with the emergence of at least one real person. The fuel that supplies the growth and evolution of a relationship is the real self and only the real self. The strategic self keeps the system stuck in habitual patterns; the real self necessarily evolves the system.

> The fuel that supplies the growth and evolution of a relationship is the real self and only the real self. The strategic self keeps the system stuck in habitual patterns; the real self necessarily evolves the system.

In Duane's case, he unconsciously waited for Catherine to return from her walkabout into the playing field and pick up where she left off: taking care of the relationship, or overfunctioning. He kept looking across the living room and the bed and wondering when she would come to her senses.

She stayed in, practiced doing 100% of only her 50%, and didn't take the bait. We often say that the task is to be different even if the other(s) is the same. The pattern has to adjust in some way if one person refuses to move.

After two days, culminating in his 15 minutes of reflection, Duane finally turned to Catherine and became emotionally responsible and vulnerable. He confessed that he had been punishing her for loving him, for getting too close to his SOS, making her the explanation for the problem in the relationship. He was remorseful and accountable for his part in the crazy drama. Duane stepped in and he stayed in. (The story continued, but that is for another book on intimate relationships!)

Look around
The last step to integrate it all is to begin to look around at this new territory, this brave new world. Who am I here? Who is the other, truly? What else is here? Who else is here? Take a new picture of reality. So often in our work in workshops or private therapy there will be a moment of breakthrough or expression where the person shows an aspect of themselves—like honesty, laughing, yelling, dancing, or singing on the playing field—and then apologizes or laughs at what they just did, in effect, reinstalling the mask as quickly as possible.

In many ways, this last step of looking around requires us to move through a bit of an identity crisis. In order to enter into—and then remain on—the playing field, you must decide who you are, and choose behaviours consistent with that. You have to be willing to be you, raw and exposed, to take in the view. The view is the new information. Take a picture. Running through the door for a quick peek can allow you to have a brief new experience, but staying in and looking around allows that new experience to integrate. New information is essential to re-establish who you are now, who is actually in front of you, what actually is happening, and, ultimately, the experience that awaits us all beneath these layers of defence: the friendly universe.

Duane:

When I finally entered the playing field of my relationship with Catherine, I noticed a woman who loved me, and a man who deserved and was worthy of love. What a concept! I noticed beauty, extraordinary beauty, in her eyes that gave a blinding and brilliant glimpse of the profound innocence in both of us. I noticed the comfort, exotic splendour, and playfulness of this playing field that was rapidly transforming into a playground. All those years of being certain that this territory was only for mayhem. So many years and so many relationships never truly realized in the terror of entering the playing field. I was home.

Looking around also then demands participation. If the appropriate behaviour for the picture I had held, of a flawed man and a controlling woman, was perpetual running and hiding, then it followed that if the picture had now changed, then so would my behavioural response to it. All behaviour is appropriate given how we see what is in front of us. The picture of safety, innocence, beauty, and connection would have me standing tall, hands in the air, proclaiming my profound and undying love for all that I am, all that we are, and all that is. I would have no problem holding her, loving her, and letting her know how deep that goes. And I don't.

For all relationships, be they primary, friends, family, or even colleagues, the process of becoming emotionally responsible in the relationship web is the same. Contain, reflect rather than reload, let go of outcome, step in through vulnerable communication (and/or asking for help), stay in by continuing to contain and doing 100% of your 50%, and look around. Take a new picture. Challenge your own fear-based mind trying to prove itself by looking beyond it. There is an infinite amount of new information that waits in the unfolding mystery of our existence.

An "enlightened master" is not a person who is omniscient and certain of the truth about all things all the time. An enlightened master is a person who bows to not knowing the truth about all things and is open to knowing more about all things all the time.

LIFE ON THE PLAYING FIELD: FRIENDSHIPS

Our friendships are interesting and multifaceted. They are critical to our sense of value. We hold them dear as one place in our lives that we can count on unconditional caring and acceptance. Our best friend is often the person who for the most part agrees with us, and conflict may be relatively rare. Both inject into the relationship web's lines and circuitry similar thoughts and beliefs about men, women, life, and who the problem is in their lives. Good friends offer analysis and solutions to each other's conflicts. Good friends will generally agree with who is the problem and thus who is the solution. That person is rarely sitting at the table. As we have seen, this is called triangling. Good friends tend to do this a lot.

Similar to the dynamics of a primary relationship or family, friendships also have their strategic relationship contract, whose purpose is to provide safety on the sidelines. Friendships want to evolve as well and can as easily go into crisis if the rules are challenged or even slightly altered. We want to depend on the status quo remaining unchanged.

Sylvie, a student of ours, and her friend Jenn meet for their regular Thursday coffee at Starbucks, a tradition that has carried on since high school.

"Oh, I'm so glad you could make it, Sylvie. It is so good to see you!" Jenn anxiously states before sitting down.

"Great to see you too, Jenn," Sylvie replies, noting a level of upset in Jenn's voice.

"I think I have had it. Tom just isn't showing up. He's hardly ever at home, is always working late, and we haven't had sex in a month. This has been going on for years. Men!"

Sylvie, feeling Jenn's despair, feels obliged to console and agree with her good friend: "I don't know how you put up with that."

"Well I don't. And I let him know it. He slept on the couch last night."

Triangling is Jenn and Sylvie's go-to foundational tool for dealing with stress. Triangling is a way of dealing with anxiety in one relationship by bringing it to another relationship. All can be blamed on him or her or this or that. If only he or she or this or that changed, then all would be good. In order to preserve the stability of this pair, they talk about problems they are having in other relationships. This becomes the rule. Not playing by this rule can severely disturb the balance and homeostasis of many friendships.

In this example, Sylvie may fear losing her friendship and worth if she were to remain neutral or curious about the plight of Tom as well as the plight of Jenn. She knows that Jenn is equal to Tom in contributing her fair share to their distant and adversarial state. Jenn is very capable of putting Tom down in front of others and perpetually threatening to leave for someone better. And yet, in order for this relationship to grow, one of the two must take the opportunity to reflect rather than just reload, to put their hand on the door and walk through to a playing field. Once on the playing field, it is equally important to stay in long enough to afford a new view of self and other, thus rewriting the messages that saturate the relationship web.

Reflect rather than reload. Contain. Sit in the anxiety. Take a look. What is going on? Who am I beyond my strategies? What is actually happening inside me? These are all directives and questions essential to supporting healing and evolution. Invite emotional responsibility.

Sylvie could stop, contain, and reflect. In so doing, she may see that she also has her own stories about men coming up short in her past or currently, and her reactive reload will offer her own evidence to support the party line of bad men. She may imagine that agreeing with Jenn will solidify the foundation of a relationship that is important to her. The coffee dialogue is predictable, with an initial surface feeling of relief and support, but beneath that there is a deeper feeling of guilt and isolation that comes with seeing self as a victim and other as perpetrator. And the cycle repeats itself, with yet more guilt in the basement that doesn't want to be felt and thus even more need to have yet another coffee to find someone to blame for this lousy feeling.

Reflecting allows Sylvie to appreciate that their relationship can handle some honesty and responsible disclosure, as well as some compassion for those perpetually blamed. Prior to this moment, she hasn't rewound her own tape from her own relationship with Mario, which recently ended, to look at her involvement in its collapse. Watching Jenn launch her diatribe, Sylvie sees herself; she realizes that Mario may have wondered whether he was just a defective failure, unable to deliver her happiness, who gave up on himself before he gave up on the relationship. Maybe he was hurting. She was hurting as well but would never talk about it, instead covering it with anger and tossing it his way. Maybe she needs to take some responsibility.

She steps in:

"I wonder what Tom is going through?"

Jenn seems shocked that Sylvie dares to see anything other than Tom being at fault.

"You know, Jenn, we've know each other for so very long. All the way back to high school. You are so important to me. When I hear you speak about Tom that way, it is easy for me to agree, because that is how I felt about Mario. But you know, I played a part in that as well. I was very controlling and rejected him a lot for the same reasons as you. Underneath it all, I feared I wasn't worth being loved. I didn't talk about that. Instead I talked about how he didn't love me properly. I think he was scared of me. I know he has his part, but I have mine. I wish I had been able to talk about that. I miss him. I often wonder what he went through. I wonder the same about Tom."

It only takes one. Sylvie reflected and contained. She sat in her anxiety instead of running with it, and entered the playing field. She let go of outcome. Jenn may or may not step in to meet her. As wonderful as it would be for that to happen, it does not have to happen for change to occur. The relationship circuitry lines are rattling with new life, new thoughts, and new possibilities. If Jenn stands up and storms out of the café, never to talk again, or she jumps on Sylvie's lap in tears, they will still be in relationship. The relationship has changed. It is never the end of the story, only the end of a chapter.

If Jenn did leave the café upset, it would remain incumbent upon Sylvie to stay on the playing field as she is greeted once again with her own anxiety about losing her friend. There is an equal push back from the strategic self to run back to the old contract, apologize, and return things back to normal. In order to stay on the playing field, our ability to hang on to ourselves must keep pace with our level of anxiety. This is not only where we grow, it is the only time we can grow.

It is important to note that in all relationships when one reflects, contains, and steps in to face one's own lesson (challenging fears in the basement), a knock occurs on the door of the other's basement as well. It doesn't mean the other will answer, but at least one person has, and so the system must change. The relationship is becoming more of what it truthfully is and longs to become, which is a vehicle for evolution on the playing field, rather than a comfort zone on the sidelines. This is true whether it looks like that or not, whether there is any contact or not. We are always in relationship, and the change has not only occurred, it is felt.

Sylvie must stay in and look around and ask herself some questions: "Who is this now? What else is here? Who is everyone else? Am I just a victim who needs to guard against the bad ones, or is there more to me and to them? Who was Mario? Do I need to make amends?" She may notice that she is alive on this playing field. She may notice that all the peace and love she hoped to achieve by being the compliant, victimized strategic self on the sidelines she can actually experience by being her real self on the playing field. The playing field is the last place we look but the only place to look for what we truly are looking for. Sylvie took a new picture.

David has maintained all his close friendships from high school for over 20 years. His best friend is Mary, who supported him when he came out as gay in Grade 11. Among their circle, Mary is starting to feel left behind because everyone is married, with David the last to commit to his partner, Lucas. Most of their mutual circle also have children. David and Mary have had long conversations about Mary's pain and disappointment in where she has ended up in life. Ever since high school, David has been Mary's "counsellor," offering advice and support to Mary as needed.

When David first started our work, he quickly realized

how much he had founded his identity on overfunctioning and caretaking in order to avoid having to look at how vulnerable he actually felt inside. David was sexually abused by his father as a child and carried a deep-seated suspicion that he was not good enough. He did not go to his mother with this until much later in life, because as a child he felt the precarious nature of their marriage and tried to protect it. The strategic self he evolved to defend against his basement was to be a caretaker in all his relationships.

David's friendship had already taken an evolutionary leap when one day he refused to give advice to Mary in response to her request to "tell me what to do." Instead he said, "You know, I am not going to do that, because I actually don't know what is best for you." Mary was initially quite angry with this, but David hung in there and hung on to himself, and the relationship evolved along with him.

Then David and Lucas, after many conversations about the subject, decided to adopt a child. He was quite anxious, as the process was complicated and his family history made him worry about his own ability to parent. On top of this anxiety, he was anxious about telling Mary because he was aware that she was in a downward spiral. In his words, he found himself "tiptoeing around our friendship" and strategizing how he could tell Mary with the least possible impact. He had a dinner booked for Mary's birthday, and because he didn't want to "ruin" that event, he decided to text beforehand with a "light" announcement inviting Mary to be excited about being an honorary aunt. Mary texted back saying, "I was already having a bad day, and you just made it worse." Mary ended up cancelling the birthday dinner.

David came into our office in distress, wondering what to do about his situation with his best friend. As we discussed the situation, it became apparent that David was very attached to keeping his friendship (understandably enough), and because he was attached to that outcome, he fell back into his old pattern of caretaking. Instead, he could have stepped forward honestly and vulnerably with Mary, saying something like "I am really anxious to tell you this news because I'm afraid it will add to your pain, but I am also struggling. We are going to be parents. I'm really happy about it! But also really worried about it, and worried about how you will feel, because you are really important to me." This is an example of what doing 100% of your 50% looks like. Saying those words would have conveyed a sense of trust on a relationship level, whereas "tiptoeing around the friendship" conveyed a sense of distrust.

That opportunity was, of course, gone. But it is possible to rewind the tape. When he left our office, he intended to go back to Mary and confess, "You know, Mary, I was so worried about the impact the news of our impending parenthood would have on you that I didn't even share what I was going through. Sometimes I fall back into just focusing on you, which isn't fair. This process has actually been quite hard and stressful already, and I could really use some help from my best friend. You've said the news is hard for you, and I understand—thanks for your honesty. I also wanted to give you the opportunity to hear what is going on for me honestly, so let me know if you'd like to talk more about that."

It is painful for David to contemplate losing his long-term friendship, but the cost of hanging on to a relationship with a caretaking-wounded bird contract is harmful to both of them. David is determined to learn how to consider himself as well as others in his relationships, which requires inserting himself into the mix.

Chapter Seven

Life on the Playing Field: Family

In this session, David confessed, "There is a reason why I never charged my dad or told his new wife what happened." David continues to abide to some extent by the contract he formed with his father when he was a child, caretaking him at the expense of himself. He found some sense of value as a child by holding the secret of his abuse and being his dad's confessor and advisor when he would unload. When David considers holding his father responsible, he feels overwhelming guilt, even though he knows intellectually that this is his father's problem and responsibility, not his.

He has not had contact with his father for many years and, as an adult, has shared his story with his mother and siblings. In that sense, David has broken the secrecy surrounding his abuse and alleviated his shame. As part of the therapeutic process, David's mother has taken responsibility and apologized to David for not being present enough to notice and protect him as a young boy.

Dealing with sexual abuse within a family system is a delicate and often lengthy process because the abuse takes place in relationships where there is a strong family bond. The one who has been hurt will often act to their own detriment to preserve that bond, by maintaining secrecy or by "forgiving" or understanding too soon. In that way, they can end up reinforcing the dysfunctional relationship contracts in a new form, rather than helping the system to evolve. Describing this process in detail is beyond the scope of this book, but it is important to note that sexual abuse is far more frequent than most people assume, and the family repercussions last for generations without intervention.

Because David's behaviour with his friend was so tied

to what he'd learned in his family, we asked about his father. Apparently, several months ago his stepmother (his father's new wife) had gotten in touch with one of the other siblings, stating that David's father wanted "to make amends." David hadn't responded because the contact was so indirect. We suggested he respond simply with "What would he like to make amends for?" Even this simple communication is at a relationship level, returning the responsibility back through the relationship web to the father rather than having David continue to hold it in his silence. David found this suggestion freeing.

Stepping in on the playing field in the face of anxiety does not always require articulating emotional transparency, nor is it always appropriate. Vulnerable actions do not always require vulnerable words. But the integrity of being on the playing field requires that you let yourself be and feel vulnerable where you actually are vulnerable. Entering the state of vulnerability might mean doing less rather than more, or saying less rather than more.

Ted, a client of ours, recently spoke about a family birthday dinner he attended for his only sister, Sally. He mentioned that the family rules held him as the person who would be responsible for social flow at the dinner table. This was a family that cared about each other but could never actually vocalize any tender thoughts. Family members rarely engaged in displays of love or affection; they would tend more towards mocking it.

This was also a family that had a history of loss, frequent divorces, and family feuds. As a result, the family was not active in typical family rituals, initiating contact only in what felt like mandatory Christmas and birthday get-togethers. Superficiality was the family rule in order for family members to avoid feeling the pain around their losses and sad history. The relationship message underlying the overt communication was "When is this over? I don't care about anyone here. You don't get to choose your family; we are stuck with each other."

The moment that there was a slight lull in the conversation, Ted would feel immense pressure to ensure that the family didn't have the experience of not having anything to talk about. As Woody Allen once remarked, "If you are not busy with the little things, you have to worry about the big things." Small talk remained critically important to keep engaged and moving, undoubtedly to not fall into that more painful feeling of how sad the family had become. He had developed as his strategic mask a personality that could juggle topics and crack jokes, meanwhile also waiting for the event to be over. We encouraged Ted to let go of his strategy and let the anxiety in the family surface.

During the next gathering, after a conversation on a subject naturally concluded, Ted let it happen—silence. He left it there. Didn't speak. Just sat in the silence. He also didn't look down. He kept looking ahead, having direct eye contact. He thought he would die leaving it there. According to him, the tension at the table was nuclear.

He stepped in by reflecting rather than reloading. His stepping in was actually stepping out of overfunctioning and back to his 50% line. This was the playing field, entering the relationship web and posting a different message, changing the former judgmental relationship message to "I trust that we can know each other. Messes are okay. I haven't been showing up. I want to know you. You are important to me. You are my family. The only one I have. I care about you. I am sad. Who I am and my love for all of you is more important than keeping this distance. I will be responsible for my own feelings and respect others by letting them feel theirs." He did this without actually saying a word.

Remember, the relationship message is conveyed whether we are giving it words or not: we cannot not communicate. Legitimately contemplating those vulnerable reflections will be felt not just by the individual but also by the family.

Ted stayed in by containing and feeling his anxiety rather than letting the anxiety direct him. It was time to look around. He noticed others stirring about, looking up at him. The system was shaking and the relationship lines pulsating, searching for the comfortable distance. According to him, this lasted for 20 seconds, which felt like eternity. Ted felt like there was an opening to now to get real himself. He looked around and looked inside. Rather than cracking a joke, he told the table how important everyone was to him. In particular, he told Sally, his only sister, why she was important to him as a sister—that he loved her, was sorry that he had been avoiding the family, and wanted to be an active uncle in his niece and nephew's lives. Words like this were never spoken.

There were a few obligatory chuckles suggesting that this gesture was silly, all coming his way in a systemic attempt to get him back to the comfortable, familiar position and posture. But there were also tears in his mother's eyes and a feeling of relief at the table, now that someone was putting kind words to a difficult situation. Ted hung on to himself and further stated that he was tired of not letting his family know how important they all were to him and that he wanted to get together more often.

Giving your vulnerability words can never be argued when you are only talking about yourself. When you are only talking about yourself, it is very difficult for others to deny. When the relationship message is this responsible—meaning someone is telling the truth—the relationship often naturally relaxes, despite it feeling unusual and out of the box. At a very deep level of all of our being, we all long to be real.

Again, the victory for Ted is that he remained the real Ted. Anything that happens after that is a bonus. In his case, something shifted on the playing field in the lines of connection that was now part of the family relationship web. People in his family felt something. This cannot be erased. Ted can now be Ted anytime he wants.

Had Ted just remained silent while the family scurried about looking for another filler topic, it would have been enough to plant seeds on the playing field. He would be hanging on to himself, even if he wasn't ready to speak honestly. He is being different when the others are being the same, and not relying on others to be different in order for him to be different. On the playing field the relationship web has changed, because Ted is part of the relationship web regardless of what anyone else does in response.

Catherine:

Parenting is probably the toughest job on the planet because as your child grows and develops, they will inevitably knock on the door to your basement and challenge every SOS you have. Overall, I feel I have done a great job parenting my now adult daughter, Erin. Of course I wasn't perfect, but early on I realized that it wasn't my job to protect Erin from difficulty, it was my job to help her learn to move through difficulty. My spoken relationship contract with Erin was "Our love can handle anything," which meant that we could talk about anything and work through anything, trusting our love for each other.

Perhaps not surprisingly, I am experiencing more of a challenge now that Erin has reached adulthood. I am no longer needed in my role as Mom, at least not in a central way. I am facing with Erin the same dilemma I faced with Duane: If I am not needed, will I be wanted? If I am not necessary in her life in a concrete way, will I be welcome? What emerges from my basement is my fear of not being good enough for friends in the schoolyard as a child. I can feel the impulse to re-establish my importance as Mom to protect that fear, but have instead chosen to step in by communicating vulnerably.

Erin was intimately involved in editing this book, and I am very transparent in this book! Even though Erin is personally familiar with our work and way of relating and has heard many of these personal stories, it is another thing to essentially lay myself open to her feedback. I get scared that she will not like me. Instead of being pushed around by my fear, I am trusting in our relationship contract—that our love can handle anything we bring to it—and have let her in to my basement. Our relationship is evolving, and I am discovering that is a beautiful thing!

Duane:

Given my travel schedule and sharing the parenting duties half-time with her other family, the amount of hands-on time for the most basic of parenting duties fell more into Catherine's lap than mine. I recall one afternoon being on pick-up duty at school when Erin was probably eight or nine years old. It was a rainy and cold day. Erin burst out onto the schoolyard, hardly taking the time to notice me. She was more concerned with having a few moments racing with her friends in the rain than finding her way to the car. I had worked in child care in the early part of my career and felt called upon to assert my role as a caregiver. I was trained to establish healthy parameters for a child and protect them from danger, as well as helping them get their priorities straight. In this instance, she should put her jacket on and stay dry. I called out to her to do just that and she ignored me. I was slightly insulted by the notion and raised my voice, insisting she put on her jacket. She continued to ignore me.

Eventually we found our way to the car—not talking, but with a fair amount of fumes coming out of my ears. She ran into the house. I sat Catherine down and explained to her that we had a problem. Erin would have to accept my role as a parent in these situations, and I wanted her support. She called Erin in. I looked at her and melted. Rather than becoming the stern taskmaster, I told her that I wasn't sure who I was sometimes in this family. I told her that I wasn't a biological parent, that I didn't need to be her dad because she already had one, but that at times like this I was a little lost and not sure who I was or how I fit into all of this. Erin looked at me and stunned me. With tears in her eyes, as well as mine, she rushed over to me and said, "You are my one and only Duane."

In the end, the playing field is not a new territory. This is a very ancient one. We are not going forward so much as returning to where we came from, where we started in our original spiritual connection with the friendliness of this universe, our existence, and our emotional, psychological connection with important others.

LIFE ON THE PLAYING FIELD: WORK

The workplace presents a more complex situation, with many more moving parts, but the principles at play are the same. Most workplace problems are relational problems, and are at the root of staff morale issues, sick days, and low productivity. Despite the fact that many organizations engage in "team-building" exercises, we don't know how to address the deeper dynamics at the root of these dilemmas.

No matter how a company or organization is overtly structured, there will be a different structure that evolves out of how people relate to each other. The people who end up being psychological leaders in an organization may not be the designated leaders and may not, in fact, be working with the designated leader's direction. This is not out of bad or even conscious intention. Every workplace relationship is a two-way relationship of influence where each is having an equal impact on the other, no matter what the apparent power structure. How the organization adjusts to these dynamics determines its underlying structure.

Most of us want to feel passionate about our work because we recognize how much time and energy we will spend in the workplace. In fact, the amount of time spent in close contact with a fellow worker or workers can be more than many spend with those at home. However, as personal investment in the workplace increases, so does vulnerability, because when something is important, we feel vulnerable. This can happen when the cause we are working for is important, it can happen because the people we work with become important, and it can happen just because of the amount of time we end up spending at the workplace, as routine integrates more deeply into our lives.

As vulnerability increases, so do organizational and relational problems, because we don't know how to handle our own vulnerability. We feel vulnerable and react to our own vulnerability in predictable ways, by hiding, pretending, strategizing, and defending. The longer you spend on the job and the more passionate you feel about your work, the more your future is felt to be at the mercy of the powers that are above you and around you.

Over time, the strategic self walks ahead of the SOS into the workplace, ready for surviving another Groundhog Day at the office. Many of us approach our workplace with trepidation and fear that we believe is caused by tense situations outside ourselves; in fact, these tense situations are now being fed by the very fear and trepidation we are bringing to them.

Our client Simon was considering leaving his job due to a difficult workplace relationship. He had accepted a position at this advertising firm because he adored their focus on quality and integrity in the sales field rather than a hard-sell approach. The team worked primarily in pairs, with a graphic designer being matched up with someone tasked with coming up with the larger creative vision. They were expected to collaborate on projects together. Sarah was the creative ideas person and Simon the hands-on graphics man. In Simon's mind, Sarah was far too involved in what he considered his territory, undermining his ability to do his job.

He described an incident where he was finalizing a piece but struggling to remember how to merge two images together for a certain effect. Sarah was "once again looking over his shoulder." It drove him crazy. She noticed him being stuck and started making a suggestion of a workaround. He lost it. He wasn't very demonstrative most of the time, but in this instance he replied with a raised tone, "I've got it, Sarah," not allowing her to complete her thought. He followed this with "I know what I'm doing. Why don't you do your job and I'll do mine?"

Sarah was taken aback and visibly hurt. "Fine, do it yourself, then!" Sarah snapped back. She stormed back to her chair, turning her back on him. The silence and the distance that followed was unbearable, on the one hand, but very familiar on the other. They were both back home. Typically, their strategic selves would play this out and replicate the lives they came from.

As in every case of conflict, we are not upset for the reasons that we think. We have successfully re-enacted scenes from our past that have not resolved themselves, and we are now playing them out again in the present. After some discussion, it became apparent what SOS and past issue was being triggered in Simon. We spoke of various ways to be emotionally responsible, and he ended up choosing what felt like the greatest risk: to become vulnerably transparent with Sarah.

It only takes one to step in. The day after our session, following a few minutes of silent torture, Simon turned his chair towards Sarah and asked if she had time to talk about what had happened. She reluctantly agreed, looking at her watch as if she might have other things to attend to that were more important than him. He replied by thanking her and went on to say, "Sarah, I am sorry first for my tone and what I just said to you. I seriously want to have a great working relationship with you. I should let you know a bit about me. I often doubt myself and wonder if there is anything I really do well, including this."

Sarah responded, "Are you kidding me? I didn't know that."

"This is one area of my life I am paid to do well and it is so important to me to know maybe, just maybe, I might mean something and matter. My older brother was always good at everything. Got all the praise. He was a natural at everything. A lot like you. I watch you so easily just fly with your ideas, even in areas that are not your specialty. I envy that. When you started making that suggestion, I make it mean that I am useless, and I can't stand to feel that, so I barked at you and made you the problem. I am sorry for that. You were actually right with your suggestion! I couldn't admit it, but I am now. I'm really sorry."

Sarah's response startled him. "You know, Simon, I love working with you. I want this to work as well. And I have to say it wasn't okay for me either to snap back like that. I actually think you do great work. I just wanted to help. In no way was

I thinking you were not good at what you do. I also think that I need to be needed and wonder what my worth is if I am not! I do this everywhere, messing in other people's business. I was the little mother in my house because my mother drank a lot and someone had to take care of things. I was praised for that. But I caretake far too much. Maybe this is what my husband goes through with with me?" This was actually quite a response by Sarah, because we had prepared Simon not to expect his vulnerability to be reciprocated. This example turned out as well as it possibly could have.

Simon could easily have just remained in his victim state, uploading this experience of not trusting others and reinforcing his low self-esteem. The tense silence could define this work relationship. He could either continue to deal with his anxiety by distancing and talking behind Sarah's back in the coffee room, seeking collusion with others, or with his wife at home. This sadly is the case for many of us so much of the time with those we work with.

Instead, Simon became emotionally transparent. He stepped onto the playing field by talking about himself from the basement. This was no easy task. There were no guarantees. He hung on to himself by letting go of who he thought he was supposed to be, exposing who he feared he was in order to welcome the news about who he truly was. He was being emotionally responsible by willing to be vulnerable.

Vulnerability is not guaranteed to work, as it did so beautifully for Simon, but it is guaranteed to work better than our defences. If vulnerability feels inappropriate or too risky, it is never wrong to be accountable. Simon could have had the same conversation expressing his remorse without going into details about his past by saying something like "Sarah, I'm really sorry I snapped at you the other day. In retrospect, I realize you were trying to be helpful, but I took it as a criticism at the time because I was already feeling upset with myself. I apologize."

Simon was also willing to be wrong, which is a vital ingredient in allowing something new to occur on the playing field: we must be willing to be wrong. That does not mean we are wrong, but we must enter these courageous conversations being willing to be. Hiding behind our guarded and strategic self, we believe we have all the information and have come to the right conclusion.

As was illustrated in the farmer parable, we never know everything. There is always more information. Our path to healing is the willingness to be guided by what we do not know rather than what we think we do know. Being willing to be wrong brings with it a natural curiosity for that unknown, a laying down of arms, and a relationship message that is friendly, respectful, and open.

SELF-APPLICATION

The following chart will help you walk through the kinds of situations we described above and identify how you can step through the door and onto the playing field. Taking the time to write this out formally for every trigger you run into will eventually integrate into an informal, natural process. The moment something happens and the strategic self is reloaded and ready to fire, the first step is to **stop** and contain. Give yourself this 15-minute window to reflect rather than reload. This may feel like the hardest place to reflect, but it is the most important place to reflect. As we have seen, these moments of upset are also transformation points.

Choose one of those "something happens" moments in your life that typically gets you into a reactive state and walk through each step, moving from reactivity to correction.

1. What is the trigger?
   What is the situation that fires up a reaction in you instantly?

2. What do you make it mean?
   What do you make it mean about whoever is triggering this in you, or about life itself. What SOS is confirmed by this event?

3. Just like when in your life?
   Reflect back on your personal history for the source of a similar type of situation, or "just like when."

4. What do you do when you make it mean that?
   Identify your reactive strategies, referring to the acting out/in behaviours you identified in Chapter two.

5. What is the cost when you react in this way?
   What is the result in the end of your own reactivity to this situation? Where does it leave you? Feeling what?

6. Do you actually know what it means?
   No. *The answer is always, unequivocally, no, just as in the farmer parable.*

7. What might it actually mean?
   First of all, is that SOS true? If not, what is true? Widen the context. Look around. What might be happening for the other people involved? Continue looking until the situation is no longer personal and there is no longer a sense of good guys and bad guys.

8. What would you do or say if it meant that?
   What actions would naturally follow if the meanings in #7 were true?

9. What is the benefit of seeing the situation this way and behaving this way
   How does your new proactive behaviour enhance and improve your life?

8 THE REAL WORLD

*The universe is filled with magical things, patiently waiting
for our wits to grow sharper.*
—Eden Phillpotts

*You yourself, as much as anybody in the entire universe,
deserve your own love and affection.*
—Buddha

IS THE UNIVERSE A FRIENDLY PLACE OR NOT?

Catherine:

*I had an experience in 1994 that completely transformed my world
view, during the birth of my daughter, Erin. I remember saying
that I wanted the birth of my child to be "meaningful." Anyone ever
told you "be careful what you wish for"?*

*Now, had you asked me at the time whether I believed the
universe was a friendly place, I would have said, "Yes, absolutely."
My behaviour belied that statement, however, as I was a control*

freak. Nowhere was this more evident than in my birthing process.

I had studied childbirth manuals diligently and had been set on as natural a birth experience as I could have, in a birthing centre with a midwife. After 40 hours of attempting just that, I had been rushed to hospital, where I was hooked up to all kinds of monitoring machines. My labour was not progressing as it should, and it was decided to help the process along with an oxytocin drip. The drip certainly intensified my contractions, with one coming on top of another, but it didn't help, as they never became even and progressive the way the books said they should. I was starting to feel scared.

No one knew that, however. Whenever a nurse or doctor asked how I was doing, I assured them I was fine. In fact, the sum total of outward evidence of my distress was a few tears and my husband's crushed hand. That was it. No noise.

About 50 hours in, it finally dawned on me how much I was attempting to control the process, particularly the pain, rather than surrendering to it. I started, with each breath, telling myself to "surrender, let go."

It helped. A strange thing happened: the nature of my suffering changed the more I was able to accept it rather than control it. "Pain is inevitable. Suffering is optional." This was my first hint of what Haruki Murakami meant, and it informs much of our subsequent work.

I was in active labour for four hours and got into serious trouble, in part because I was exhausted and unwilling to admit it. In the end, my daughter was stuck (shoulder dystocia) and it was too late to do a Caesarean. There was a violent intervention, and finally Erin was born. I remember seeing her for no more than a minute, on my stomach, as the cord was cut. She was blue, and was immediately whisked off to intensive care.

I started to hemorrhage. My usually calm, collected doctor began *to scream at the nurses, and people were running everywhere. There was panic and commotion around because (as I later found out) it was a busy night on the ward and someone had forgotten to get blood matched and ready for me when I'd turned into a high-risk case.*

In that moment, in that hospital bed, hooked up to all those machines, with doctors and nurses attempting to staunch the blood flow, I realized I was dying. I realized there was no such thing as control.

And I'm not sure what happened next.

I just know that I completely let go.

And what followed was a moment that redefined my entire life. I experienced a state beyond anything I could ever imagine or describe adequately on paper. "So this is what it means to let go of control!" was my thought. For the first time in my life, I felt completely filled with what I can only call Love. It wasn't the emotion "love" that I had experienced up to this point in my life; it was an expansive, fully connected, joyful state.

I remember turning to my husband, who was still by my side, and saying, "It's okay." I didn't mean that I would be okay, I meant that it was okay no matter what happened. I experienced the friendliness of the universe, and I felt it saying, "It's okay, no matter what." I was and am a part of that, and I experienced, just for an instant, the whole. I have never felt as connected as I did in that moment, to everyone and everything. It changed forever how I see myself in relation to that greater whole.

I got what I wished for, indeed.

There has been much written about experiences such as this. In 1975 there was a study done for the US National Institute of Health on the very few survivors of those who had attempted suicide by jumping off the Golden Gate Bridge. These survivors reported very similar mystical experiences, and how they saw themselves, others, and the world was similarly transformed. They were no longer suicidal. This method of transformation, in fact, is pretty much 100% guaranteed, but unfortunately at the cost of a 2% survival rate!

The only way to answer Einstein's powerful question for ourselves, to reveal the friendliness of the universe, is to consistently let go of our control strategies (yes, all strategies are about control) and take note of who we are and what happens when we do. When we are brave enough to be our real selves, we will necessarily make contact with the real world. That world isn't perfect, and neither are we, but within even the most difficult moments there is a capacity for love and beauty that reveals itself over and over again, particularly when we look for it. When we are brave enough to extend vulnerability and love to those around us (rather than fear and defence), we contribute to the ongoing manifestation of the friendly universe.

> When we are brave enough to extend vulnerability and love to those around us (rather than fear and defence), we contribute to the ongoing manifestation of the friendly universe.

THE DOOR TO LOVE OPENS WITH GIVING

To paraphrase the Beatles, in the end the love you receive is equal to the love you give. Most people come to a workshop with the idea of becoming more effective in having their individual needs met in life, including in the workshop itself. However, the joyous and celebratory state common to the workshop experience has very little to do with whether the participant had their needs met. It has much more to do with actually relinquishing individual needs and having this need surpassed by the love affair of seeing another's interests as the same as one's own.

As the group welcomes the unique stories of those attending and trust of each other gets established, a glimpse into someone's vulnerability takes place. Much like the family we described earlier that, as a rule, bounced around in small talk to avoid a deeper conversation, a group coming together initially presents with the same level of distrust, fear, and uncertainty. Then one speaks with their hand on the door with vulnerability. It only takes one. The room always wakes up and leans forward in their chairs. All eyes are riveted to vulnerability. There is nothing in this world that can exceed the rapture of this initial awakening into the world of vulnerability revealing the ultimate prize: our collective soul. In the workshop experience, we discover that the healing power of extending care and love is equivalent to that of receiving it.

The Human Potential Movement is and has been from the outset predominantly dedicated to the cause of individual self-actualization, from which it is assumed healthy relationships will follow. In the wake of Freud's lead in the early part of the twentieth century, psychology established its focus on understanding the human condition almost strictly by the internal drives within the individual human psyche itself.

On the other side of the spectrum, Carl Jung widened the context by including the collective unconscious. He likened us to the rhizome plant that has many apparently different flowers sprouting through the ground, appearing separate and individual while below the surface they are all part of a common root system and actually make up one plant, not many. Jung may have been the first to consider this more spiritual context to fully understand the behaviour and dynamics of the human psyche. Jung believed that we all share in a journey of transformation, and it is this that is at the mystical heart of all religions. It is a journey to meet the self and at the same time to embrace the divine. Jung believed that spiritual experience was essential to our well-being.

In the 1950s Family Systems Theory was introduced, based on the principles of General Systems Theory. A family systems approach argues that in order to understand an individual within a family, we must look at the family as a whole, as the relationship context in which a person lives (past and present) is constantly shaping who they are. A common analogy used by family systems theorists and practitioners is found in baking. The cake that comes out of the oven is more than the eggs, flour, oil, baking soda, and vanilla that make up the parts or elements of the cake. It is how these elements combined to form something larger than the ingredients that makes the cake. Such is true with families as well. It is more than who makes up a family: it is how they come together and interact that defines that family.

This analogy as it applies to families comes from the General Systems Theory principle of wholeness, which states that everything is connected and cannot be understood in isolation. The whole is greater than the sum of its parts. Sounds almost mystical, doesn't it? Psychology has continued to evolve towards a greater understand of relationship (or "attachment") as vital to human well-being, but it tiptoes with some trepidation towards extending this into a spiritual ("friendly universe") dimension.

A Course in Miracles arrived in both of our lives in around 1990 (before we met in 1996), and although we have different reactions to the language, as well as some content, we were both moved by the unique interplay between the psychological and spiritual themes of the book. One of the basic tenets of the ACIM material (as well as other spiritual traditions) is the notion that what we do to another, we do to ourselves: that we are inexplicably connected both to each other and to the divine at all times. This revelation inspires a level of responsibility both to self and other that, once recognized, cannot be forgotten or avoided. Attempts to eliminate our longing to connect and our innate desire to return to a collective state of caring for each other, as part of an overall treatment strategy, will fall well short in their therapeutic results.

We are beginning to realize that we are not separate. We are beginning to realize that pursuing our individual goals in life will never lead to happiness, because we are not just individuals. We are always in relationship. We cannot fool ourselves or pretend that you or I are separate rhizome plants all by ourselves, only impacting self. Everything we do impacts others because we are connected and one. We will never find happiness by pursuing our individual goals, with the endless artillery of defence, strategy, control, and judgement, winning at the expense of another. It will never be true that happiness will come in that manner. Happiness cannot come by attacking another, any more than good health will come by removing a limb where there is pain.

We will feel guilt and we won't know why. We will feel depressed and won't know why. Beneath the conclusion that we are alone is an undying desire to be connected, to care for each other, and to return home.

> Into my heart an air that kills
> From yon far country blows:
> What are those blue remembered hills,
> What spires, what farms are those?

That is the land of lost content,
I see it shining plain,
The happy highways where I went
And cannot come again.
—A.E. Housmen

There have been a number of studies designed to measure happiness as it relates to "getting" and "giving" that clearly illustrate that giving increases our happiness. In one of these studies, the first group was given a certain amount of money with the directive to spend it wherever they desired. Another group was given the same amount of money with the directive to spend it on others. An inventory was subsequently conducted measuring levels of contentment and happiness. The group that gave to others felt measurably better. The better feeling had nothing to do with getting anything back in a concrete way.

Once on the playing field, vulnerability is not the final destination. Becoming vulnerable is the last step towards unveiling a pristine view of the innocent, connected, natural state beneath our fears about who we are. We are all perfectly imperfect, good enough, and loveable, flaws and all. When the Navajo weave a blanket, they deliberately weave a flaw into it, because they believe this allows the spirit of the blanket to roam. This is a beautiful metaphor for who we are, as well: our flaws have their own inherent beauty and allow our spirits to roam.

Once this clear view of self and others has been established, considering another's interests as not separate from our own is a natural outcome. How could it not be? As *A Course in Miracles* states, all behaviour is a call for love or an extension of it. This becomes the only possible way of viewing each other once we reach a state of vulnerability. The relationship web will never be the same.

We thus have a responsibility to maintain, protect, and mind the store of loving thoughts and actions on the playing field. We are all in this together—always have been and always will be. The love we give is what we will, in turn, experience or receive.

WHO YOU ARE (REAL OR STRATEGIC) DETERMINES HOW YOU FEEL

The way you feel is not a result of what happens to you as an adult, it is a result of what you bring to each situation you encounter. You are the first cause of your own life experience. You always have been. This doesn't mean you have the power to determine what other people say or do, or that you have the power to magically create the life you think you need; it means that what you give, authentically, is what you get to experience.

Difficult things happen in life. People we love die, sometimes in tragic circumstances. Pain is inevitable, but who you are while you are dealing with what life puts in front of you is everything. We have all been inspired by stories of people who rise to become their best selves out of the worst circumstances. Who are you in the middle of what life hands you? Are you the same person if life is good or bad?

As you become more and more aware of your own masks and defences, you begin to realize that perception when hiding behind your mask is a mirror reflecting back to you your own evaluation of self. When you are operating out of strategy and defence, you are collecting evidence to prove your fear. You see what you are looking for and react to that. As you drop your defence and step forward, vulnerably and curiously, you are opening to new possibility. Perception becomes a window through which new information can enter. You enter the real world by being willing to be real yourself.

Taking responsibility for our own experience is an empowering opportunity. Who you are and what you naturally extend to others on the playing field will come back to you and determine how you feel. Once connection is made by revealing the basement of your psyche and correction occurs with a new self-evaluation, this celebration of self will just happen. You will feel good. A party breaks out on the playing field.

In the same way that operating from strategy and control will naturally produce the very bad feeling it is trying to get rid of, operating from vulnerability on the playing field will produce the good feeling we long for. Extending this trusting and loving self produces more of itself just by the sheer act of giving it. The awakened Scrooge in *A Christmas Carol* comes to mind as a great example of this principle.

CHANGING HOW YOU RELATE TO THE PAST CHANGES HOW YOU RELATE TO THE PRESENT

It is difficult these days to walk through a bookstore or log on to Amazon.com without running into new literature advocating the notion of letting go of the past in order to achieve some sort of happiness in the present. "Be here now." We don't agree. It is important to let go of your version of the past. It is your version that is causing all the problems.

It is important to let go of your version of the past. It is your *version* that is causing all the problems.

A Course in Miracles tells us that the only thing that is valuable in the past is the love that was there, and all else must be forgotten. In that sense, if the version of the past that you carry is not the version that has love as its central theme and conclusion, then something is off and you will suffer. In the same way that we must reconnect to self by changing our minds about who we are, we must reconnect with our own life stories by changing our minds and hearts about who those people were, and are, as well. Falling in love with your story is required for connecting to yourself, because your story has shaped who you are.

Duane:

My relationship with my father, Paddy, as described earlier, was frequented with terrible bouts of violence and abuse. This all did happen. Remembering only the love that was there does not mean we pour pink paint all over it to make it good, as Marianne Williamson so aptly described. On the contrary: on the playing field, going back to our past means re-entering—or even re-enacting— and feeling again the experience of the past in order to uncover the vulnerable story behind the bad, defended story.

Paddy was twenty-two when he met my mother, Lorraine, at fifteen. Both were young people living on farms in two separate communities in Northern Alberta. Paddy was from an Irish community and Lorraine from a French community. They met and she got pregnant fairly early on.

On those horrific nights, Paddy would accuse and punish Lorraine for ruining his life, for his not being able to pursue his talent as a baseball player. I was given the very distinct impression that Paddy was not the one who wanted to get married way back when. More, the theme was that he was forced into a shotgun wedding, their being good Catholics, and all.

I conducted an interview with my grandmother on my mother's side shortly before she died, after my father committed suicide. During this interview, it came out that Lorraine's parents had told both Paddy and Lorraine that they didn't have to get married. Lorraine could give birth to the child on the farm, and they would call Lorraine's child theirs. My grandmother was still giving birth herself; I actually have two uncles who are younger than me. They told my father he could carry on with his dream of becoming a professional baseball player. She went on to tell me that Paddy put her up against the wall, informing her and my grandfather in no uncertain terms that no one was going to get in the way of his marrying Lorraine. He loved her.

I was stunned. This was not my version of the past. I had built most of his life on the notion that Dad was bad, that men were bad. That I must be bad. Women were weak and needed to be protected from men, unwanted and powerless. My story carried with it the imperative to make up for the sins of my father. If this was not the whole story, and my survival personality was all founded on this story, then who was I now? Who was my father?

The whole wall came tumbling down. I realized that my mother, the oldest of six children at the time, was fifteen when they met, had a child and was married at seventeen, gave birth to two more, including me, before she was twenty-one, left the farm, and moved to Vancouver, over a thousand miles away from her family. I imagined what that must have been like for her. In her large family on the farm, she no doubt had hardly any time to have a childhood and was busy being a mini-mother for her siblings. Having three children before she was twenty-one did not allow her to get to know herself, have a life, grow up, or learn how to love my father. Surely she could care for Paddy to the extent that a fifteen-year-old could, but it is doubtful that Paddy ever felt the love that he so much wanted. He was older and knew what he wanted. It was she who didn't know, couldn't know. He was in pain, and he turned to drinking to medicate that pain.

By the time she was able to have any mature ability to love, my father's drinking had abolished that possibility and the game was on. The realization that changed my life forever was appreciating that Paddy was not going to the pub to conjure up new and better ways to punish Lorraine. No. The real story, or at least closer to the real story, is that Paddy was going to the pub to kill the pain inside of him. Paddy didn't know how to be vulnerable.

Changing how I saw them changed how I saw myself. If Paddy wasn't bad, maybe I wasn't either. Maybe I didn't have to be Superman any longer. Maybe I could become real, as I allowed my dad to become real. Perhaps all of us can all become more of who we are, the more we discover of who our parents and important others actually are!

In order to be truly *here and now*, we must also be willing to be there and then. The extent that we have peeled away our version of the past to reveal the heart beneath will equal our ability to experience the brilliance of the present. Otherwise, what we haven't worked out in our version of the past, we will act out in the present by diverting our attention to those triggering us in that present. Because we bring it with us, we will experience it. We cannot just "let go" of the past, as so many advise. That would be like prescribing amnesia as a treatment plan. We have to fill in the blanks and holes with the original colours and give life back to those in our past whom we have reduced to stick people, a caricature of themselves.

There has never been a good story written that goes "Once upon a time everything was perfect and they lived happily ever after." The stories that inspire us include victory and defeat, loves and losses, and, ultimately, the triumph of the human spirit. Duane's is a beautiful story filled with real people. It is a story that he can live with and live out with grace and dignity. Our collective journey requires falling in love with our own stories so that we can live them out as the heroic adventures they are meant to be.

> Our collective journey requires falling in love with our own stories so that we can live them out as the heroic adventures they are meant to be.

Central to coming to terms with traumatic events is the realization that who you are, coming out of these events, is more than you might have been if they had never happened. You survived. You are still here. And the defences you developed a result of what happened are also your gifts, tools that you can use from your real self to extend something positive to those around you, rather than using them to hide, pretend, or defend. Most of Duane's therapeutic skills came from sitting up with his father at night, de-escalating him. This is part of his heroic story.

LIFE ORGANIZES ITSELF AROUND WHO YOU PUT INTO IT

You become an expert in the world you live in and the shoes you walk in. On the playing field, you will get better at noticing people caring rather than controlling, kindness instead of condescension, or someone's call for love instead of their anger. Remember the story of Duane meeting that person on the trail ("It's a beautiful day, isn't it?" "Yes, but it's not going to last!"). Both were responding to the same sunny day. Charles Manson and Mother Teresa walking down the same street together are both witnessing what they are looking for. Life organizes itself around not only how you see it but what you then put into it.

When we are operating out of strategy and defence, we

are hiding our real selves and depriving ourselves of the state of connection that we long for. Metaphorically, it is as if we are a radio station that loves jazz music but broadcasts country and western 24-7. The world cooperates, and organizes itself around what we are putting into it. We will complain that everyone we meet is wearing a cowboy hat, but as we have seen, we ourselves were actively involved in establishing those relationship contracts.

When we are brave enough to broadcast jazz, meaning be responsible and real, then the people wearing berets will have a chance to show up. Your real life, which requires your real self to participate in it, will be and is far more rewarding, expansive, and amazing than anything you could manufacture strategically. You are in the middle of a heroic story with challenges and triumphs. You are perfectly shaped by your history for the adventure that only you can live out. Not only will you notice a wider, panoramic view of reality with a full spectrum of colours consistent with how you feel, the world will also reorganize itself around you given what you now know and believe.

Life on the sidelines isn't really life. When your hand was on the door to the basement, you hadn't met the world on the playing field yet. It was the time of blind faith, when you must be willing to let go of having safety as a goal and step into risking more. You have to first reflect and have a face-to-face with yourself, being willing to invite contact through vulnerability. With connection comes new information and a new experience. Entering the playing field is both a cognitive and an emotionally generative experience. Cognition affords you a new empirical concept of what could be, and following through with action allows a new experience. This generates more of itself by having a more inviting and friendly relationship with the world.

One of Duane's favourite experiences is going to garage sales. He will often park his car beside a driveway and start walking towards the used and discarded merchandise alongside the collection of neighbours drinking coffee who are putting on this sale. Duane will holler out, "Hi, I'm home, where's my coffee?" Almost without exception, on cue, the majority of those hosting the event, as well as those milling about, respond with something akin to "Well it's about time," "What do you take in it?" or "Just like you to show up when all the work has already been done."

On the surface, Duane's shout may appear to be lacking in respect, entitled, or even offensive, which would be true if his relationship message on the sidelines was indeed negative in intention. If that were the case, people might want to look for a baseball bat instead of a cup to pour the coffee in. But that isn't the case. Duane's relationship message is something to the effect of "My, it's good to be alive, having a day off and meeting wonderful people who are part of a community that is important to me. I love life and I love people." Duane has a special talent for sending those kinds of celebratory relationship messages.

Catherine's unique strength is leaning towards vulnerability in situations where most people would be tempted to lean away. She confesses to staff when her historic fears of being the one no one likes on the schoolyard surface, and lets people get to know her without expecting them to adjust. She has, much to the chagrin of her lawyer, insisted on putting a personal apology into the middle of a legal affidavit. Vulnerability has been the driving force in her relationship with her daughter, who affectionately refers to their "Kleenex box conversations." All of this inserts a message of trust into her relationship web.

The world responds in kind to those relationship messages.

If you truly want to get a read on what your relationship web message is, just take a look at what typically goes on around you.

YOU ARE THE WORLD

What we put into our relationships has a profound impact on the quality of our individual lives, as well as the entire planet. We only have to look as far as the headlines in our morning paper to read how our global emotional irresponsibility and lack of caring for each other has a tragic cost. The headlines offer endless competing reports of the pain, agony, death, and torture that come as a result of believing we are separate, different, and better or less than, justifying an endless fight for what little we believe we have, and the fear that someone or something else threatens to take even that away.

Einstein said we cannot solve a problem with the same consciousness that created it. We are evolving from independence towards (back to?) a genuine interdependent consciousness—not just knowing in our heads that everything is connected, but feeling that heart connection. Take a moment to consider how differently you would live your life if you felt the connection between all beings and were as aware of every action that impacts another as you are of what impacts self. Would you buy the second car or throw out that little insignificant piece of trash rather than recycling it if you were aware of the impact that every act has on the whole? How differently would you treat people, those close to you and strangers alike, if you really knew them to be joined with you in a concrete way? If we really, deeply consider the possibility, it's mind-boggling.

We get a taste of this possibility in workshops. One of the things we hear most frequently from participants is how struck they are by how everyone is really the same underneath, and how they benefit every time someone else shifts. Within the safe cocoon of a workshop, most people experience the reality of their connectedness to others and to a force both within and greater than their individual selves.

Unfortunately, our individual sense of identity feels threatened by the experience, and so we don't generalize it easily to "out there" in the world. In order to experience the profound depth of our real identities, we have to give up our separate, little, individual sense of ourselves and who we are. Yet we can't get the experience we all crave from our individual, separate state of mind. We have to expand our frame to encompass a broader vision of who we are, collectively.

The opportunity to make this choice exists in every interaction, in every moment, with every person we encounter. We are and always have been part of an elaborate and exquisite network of relationship circuits constantly uploading, downloading, and updating our relationship messages to and from each other. We have absolutely no choice whether we are part of that system or whether we are contributing to that interaction. We are, all the time, in every waking moment or sleeping state, whether we look at others walking by or whether we stop and say hello. It makes no difference if you delete someone from your Facebook account or leave them a message every day, whether you talk to your partner at the dinner table or not: you are communicating. All messages being conveyed are immediate and effective. We do not have a choice about these connections. We only have a choice in what we put into them.

We have a responsibility to ask ourselves what we are really communicating in all relationships. The 30-second contact you make with someone you are sharing a trip on the elevator with from the ground floor to the seventeenth may be your only time together in your entire life. What can be done with it? How will you connect? Will you just look at floor numbers, conveying the messages "When is this over? This is uncomfortable. You are dangerous," or "You don't exist"? Or will you maximize the uniqueness of this moment with this person by smiling or saying "Hello!" with eye contact and legitimately, silently conveying the friendly message "It is no accident you are here. I don't know you, but I am open and I truly do wish you to have a good day." This applies if you are in a courtroom working through a divorce settlement with your former partner, a politician observing a member of the opposing political party across the floor, or a delegate at the UN.

Can we step into these moments—whether in the elevator with a stranger, coming home to our partner, or everything in between—and take full responsibility for what we will use the situation for? Can we make up our mind ahead of time that all moments are an opportunity to not only visit the playing field and be the ambassador of friendly relationship messages, but also to let it become an explicit communication, converting to considerate and loving behaviour? Can we agree that this is our purpose for being here, above all else?

> The ingredients we each put into the collective mix determine the nature of the cake our human family takes out of the oven.

Life organizes itself around what we put into it. The state of the world is a result of what we are each putting into it. Your unloving, defended actions may not be as dramatic as a terrorist's, but every unloving action put into our collective system influences the whole. The ingredients we each put into the collective mix determines the nature of the cake our human family takes out of the oven. What you put into the system can have a profound impact, positive or negative, no matter how small the action.

Certainly this book is a vulnerable act, given that we are sharing ourselves transparently with people we have not had the privilege of meeting in person. We do this routinely when we give talks or workshops, but in those circumstances, we have immediate relationship feedback on what we say, which influences how we continue. Putting ourselves out in words adds another layer of vulnerability, and is therefore another demonstration of what we teach. Thank you again to our families for understanding the importance of this process to us, and particularly to our daughter, Erin, who has helped to shape this book with her word craft.

There are no moments that do not matter, count, or contribute to the quality of your personal day or the world's current state. The impact of this realization is staggering. We no longer have the luxury of lingering over the decision to take emotional responsibility. Love can no longer be an accidental state; we must cultivate it and choose to be directed by it, especially where it is difficult.

Stepping in, staying in, and looking around on the playing field will eventually bring us to the celebratory state of being in sheer gratitude for existing at all. We will be compelled to communicate our appreciation for the privilege of existing together with our friends, family, or acquaintances for the relatively short time we are here. If we dare enter this depth of open vulnerability and confess how important we all are to each other and the love that we have, it will reveal the divine and the infinite.

The lyrics below are from the song "Saturn" by the band Sleeping at Last. The song was inspired by the composer, Ryan

O'Neal, reflecting on the depth of the relationship message while dealing with a dying friend. It is a good exercise to reflect on how you would want to look back on your life if it were ending, and allow that to inform how you will live your life now. At the end of the day, love is all that matters, and to experience love, we have to risk being real.

> You taught me the courage of stars before you left.
> How light carries on endlessly, even after death.
> With shortness of breath, you explained the infinite.
> How rare and beautiful it is to even exist.
> I couldn't help but ask
> For you to say it all again.
> I tried to write it down
> But I could never find a pen.
> I'd give anything to hear
> You say it one more time,
> That the universe was made
> Just to be seen by my eyes.

Duane and Catherine O'Kane are Registered Clinical Counsellors, workshop facilitators, and entertaining public speakers who have over 60 (combined) years of experience in the helping profession. Duane and Catherine co-founded Clearmind International Institute Inc., a company that provides personal therapeutic and professional programs throughout Europe and North America. They have helped thousands of people discover the power of connection and how to "love out loud." Perhaps more importantly, Duane and Catherine practise what they preach in all their relationships (including their marriage) and share their struggles and wisdom vulnerably, with passion and humour.

Workshops

1-800-210-0372
workshops@clearmind.com
www.clearmind.com/index.php/workshops-2.html

Leadership Development

604-444-7477
marketing@clearmind.com
www.clearmind.com/index.php/engaging-your-organization.
html

Speaking Engagements

catherine.okane@clearmind.com
www.clearmind.com/index.php/connecting-with-your-
community/speaker-series.html

Counselling

1-800-210-0372
alumni@clearmind.com
www.clearmind.com/index.php/2016-06-28-20-13-20/
counsellor-training-alumni.html

Satellite Contacts

www.clearmind.com/index.php/about/our-team.html

Social Media

Facebook: www.facebook.com/ClearmindInternational
YouTube: www.youtube.com/user/TheClearmindChannel
Instagram: www.instagram.com/clearmind_international
Twitter: twitter.com/clearmind_intl
Pinterest: www.pinterest.com/CMIcatherine/

CPSIA information can be obtained
at www.ICGtesting.com
Printed in the USA
LVOW04s1000201116
513798LV00010B/815/P